Welcome to Successful Investing!

Dick A [illegible]

THE COMPLETE INVESTOR'S GUIDE TO SILVER DOLLAR INVESTING

The Complete Investor's Guide to Silver Dollar Investing

Dick A. Reed

The English Factory
Phoenix

Published by

The English Factory
2015 N. 37th Place
Phoenix, Arizona 85008

ISBN: 0-911349-00-6

Library of Congress Catalog Card Number: 82084121

Manufactured in the United States of America

ACKNOWLEDGEMENTS

As with any involved project, this book is the result of the combined efforts of a number of people who assisted in various stages of its organization and production. I would particularly like to thank the following people and institutions for their valuable assistance in this project:

Patrick Walsh and the staff of New Age Type and Graphics of Tempe, Arizona who provided typesetting and mechanical art services;

Malcolm Marr and the staff of Imperial Litho/Graphics of Phoenix, Arizona for their excellent and timely production of the book;

My editor, Ken Bacher, for his professional assistance throughout the course of the past years in research, as well as editing and production;

The American Numismatic Association, of which I have been a Life Member since 1974, for its support and assistance, and the valuable services it continues to provide for all professional Numismatists;

My fellow professional Numismatists for their years of dedication to our shared profession;

and last, but certainly not least, special thanks to Vickie Nicholson; to my father, Frank Reed, and to the staff of Metro Coin Limited for their assistance and support while I was dedicating much of my time to the writing and production of this book.

D.A.R.

ABOUT THE AUTHOR

Dick A. Reed is the founder and owner of Metro Coin, Ltd. of Phoenix, Arizona and a highly respected expert in silver dollar investing and numismatics in general. He is a life member of the American Numismatic Association, and has been an advisor and consultant on several previous books on silver dollar and numismatic investments.

As a silver dollar investor himself for nearly two decades, he has developed a highly successful track record for his own, and his clients', investment portfolio, and in addition is the owner of one of the world's most extensive collections of Arizona Territorial and post-Territorial Tokens, as well as other numismatic rarities.

With a degree in accounting and his extensive silver dollar experience, Dick A. Reed is a frequent advisor on numismatic matters to non-profit institutions including universities and museums. He also writes a monthly column on numismatic investing for *The Robb Report,* and publishes *Update,* a monthly newsletter for his clients.

In addition to the daily operation of Metro Coin, Ltd. and his other business interests, he travels to an average of 45 coin functions, auctions and conventions each year, and maintains the latest state-of-the-art communications and data processing equipment in his efforts to maintain his knowledge of current trends and developments in the numismatic industry worldwide.

TABLE OF CONTENTS

INTRODUCTION

The main reason for writing this book is to provide the same level of information for the investor regarding investments in silver dollars that is common among coin dealers and professional numismatists. By creating this parity of information between the investor and dealer, I can provide an overall picture of the silver dollar market, its investment potential, and the true value of silver dollars by grade and date.

While a few books have already been written on silver dollars, I was encouraged to write this book by many investors who felt the current volumes did not provide the depth of information required to make substantial investments in the silver dollar market. Therefore, areas that may not have been fully discussed in other books will be thoroughly examined from an investor's point of view in the chapters that follow.

The reason I felt confident to undertake this task is my nearly two decades of experience in the coin industry, and the discussions I have had with thousands of investors at coin shows and auctions worldwide over the years. By attending an average of 45 shows and/or auctions each year, I am in a position to better examine the silver dollar market, as well as to determine what constitutes a successful transaction from both the investor's and the dealer's point of view.

My definition of a balanced, successful transaction is one in which a dealer receives a *fair* profit for his merchandise, and leaves the bulk of potential profits to be made by the investor. This has not always been the case, whether due to misgrading, or mispricing, the lion's share of the profits have gone to the dealers. The balance I am attempting to establish in this book is that whether the investor is buying or selling, his or her assets should be protected at all times.

The obvious problem in transactions is to decide what is fair in terms of profit-potential and profit-receiving, and this is one of the areas in which my book will solve an age-old gap of understanding. Remember, no matter how good the advice is, or the recommendations given, if a coin is overpriced or misgraded, the investor will not receive the same profits as a more knowledgeable investor.

The reader will not receive an advanced degree in numismatics by reading this book, but he or she will receive enough information to make successful investment decisions regarding silver dollars, and to take advantage of their unequalled investment potential.

In the beginning of the coin marketplace, collectors, investors and coin dealers alike were satisfied to simply divide coins into circulated and uncirculated categories. Since so few people were involved at that time, this system worked fairly well. But as more people became involved in investments in silver dollars, the use of adjectives to describe various levels of uncirculated coins began. Unfortunately, this muddied the waters rather than clarifying the various levels because the adjectives used varied from person to person and dealer to dealer.

This led to the development of the Mint State numbering system, originally developed for use in establishing the value of large cents by Dr. William Sheldon, to determine the grade of a coin. These numbers range from 0 to 70. The difficulty that developed with this system was that the numbers were not used in a standardized, consistent way. The system is not at fault here; rather the accuracy of the grader is to blame for the confusion that the use of the Mint State numbers has generated in the coin industry.

Because of this, I will employ more of the Mint State grading system to rectify some of the problems that have developed in the past. This will insure the investor of accurate, standardized grading that will protect his or her investment, and make the system more understandable to everyone involved. The chapter on Grading (Chapter 4) in this book offers a pictorial review of this revised grading system.

This book will further benefit the investor and dealer, now that the difficulties of grading have been rectified, by also discussing the problems of pricing that have troubled investors and dealers alike.

This advancement is timely in that today more than 10 million people are actively involved in collecting and investing in coins; this industry is no longer a small population of investors, but a major area of investments in the United States and around the world.

Since I believe that most of these investors and collectors are attracted to silver dollars, this book will concentrate on the history and potential of the silver dollar market, though this technique of grading and pricing may be used in other areas of numismatics as well.

Historically, silver dollars have established a continuing pattern of appreciation in value, in spite of economic ups and downs, governmental actions and intervention, or the drastic price swings that the silver, gold and platinum markets have taken over the years. This upward, "Stair-step" pattern of increasing value will also be discussed in this book, as will the outline of successful silver dollar investment techniques which I have developed, both for myself, and for my clients, over the past two decades.

Dick A. Reed
Phoenix, Arizona

1

A SHORT HISTORY OF NUMISMATICS

It is sometimes difficult for those of us currently involved in the numismatic industry in the United States to remember that ours is a fairly young profession: just over a hundred years ago, coin collecting was centered in England (at least for American colonial and early United States coins), and there were only a handful of active coin collectors in the entire United States.

Most of these collectors lived around Philadelphia. While it was no longer the only U.S. Mint in operation (the San Francisco Mint had opened in 1849), it was the most productive.

Serious coin collecting in the United States had begun just after the turn of the 19th Century, and collectors were primarily interested in coins from the colonial period, although a few were also interested in very early United States coinage.

One of the first truly active coin collectors in the nation was Joseph J. Mickley, who had begun his collection with a large cent minted in the year of his birth, 1799. Mickley had something of a rough start in what was to be his long career as a coin collector: the cent he had selected was, at that time, the rarest of the entire 1793-1857 large cent series. He began his collection at the age of 17, in 1816. In that same year, a major fire occurred at the Philadelphia Mint revealing a large cache of dies from earlier U.S. coins. Mickley acquired the dies too, and his collecting began in earnest. His famous collection increased until 1867, when coins valued at more than $16,000 were stolen from his home in a burglary. A similar quantity of coins remained. Mickley had liquidated his entire collection prior to his death in 1878.

The first collector to make a business of his hobby was Edward Cogan, also a Philadelphia resident at that time, who was a dealer in books, antiques and art objects. In fact, everyone involved with coins, in those days, either simply collected them, or sold them as a side line. Cogan began collecting large cents in 1858. By the end of that year, he had collected an entire series of the large cents, and had begun to sell off his duplicates.

The 1850s and 1860s were an active period for coin collecting in the United States. Professional numismatists began to actively become involved in grading and pricing coins, and the volume of coin transactions leap-frogged from Cogan's first sale, which realized $129, to the May 1864 sale of the McCoy Collection, which brought $13,010. This was a record sale at the time, and was handled by G.A. Leavitt of New York City.

Auction houses became very involved in selling coins in this period, and catalogues were produced with very glowing descriptions of the coins in each lot. Unfortunately, not all of the coins lived up to their glowing descriptions, and Cogan became involved in several volleys of heated letters with the auction houses over these misrepresentations. Today, auctions involve very colorful catalogues, featuring photographs of the coins themselves, as well as descriptions, and they are preceeded by opportunities to view each lot of coins. However, some misrepresentations remain; especially in over-description, photographic manipulation, etc. The problems of pricing and grading also remain, as will be discussed later.

In 1866, the first issue of the *American Journal of Numismatics* was published, making it the first publication on coin collecting in the United States. The very first issue contained the first published admission that dishonesty existed in the coin business, and the editors vowed to keep a watchful eye for these "nefarious and improper acts, either in the manufacture, collection or sale of coins and medals. . . . "

Interest in coin collecting had increased substantially in the several years prior to 1858. In Cogan's opinion, this was because of the change from the old large copper cents to the new flying eagle cent design in 1856 and 1857. At the time, he estimated the entire population of serious coin collectors at about 100 people nationwide.

During this period, collectors who wanted proof coins could simply obtain them (surreptiously) from the Mint's employees. One night watchman at the Mint was reported to have produced a large number of fine proofs from existing dies of the large cents and other earlier coins while "making his nightly rounds." At one point, a few years later, even the Director of the Mint himself had a complete set of proofs of earlier coins produced for his own private collection.

Cogan would have none of it. Ever since, efforts at accurately grading and pricing coins have looked to his professional example for more than a century. In addition, he was the first to offer coins by a mail order bid, having published his first mail bid sale in November 1858.

The year 1858 was an important one in numismatics for two other very good reasons as well: First, the American Numismatic and Archeological Society was founded (the nation's first numismatic organization, whose name was changed to the American Numismatic Society some years later); and Second, the U.S. Mint began for the first time in that year to officially offer proof coins to collectors. Complete proof sets, from one cent to one dollar, sold for $3 each. It was also the first year that the term "proof" was used. Earlier, these specially-struck coins were called specimens, master coins, or presentation coins. (A proof coin is defined as a coin that is struck for a special purpose such as display or presentation.) A total of only 80 proof sets were struck in 1858.

During the Civil War, the use of paper fractional currency took the place of silver coins, but the issuance of the nickel three-cent piece (1865) and the nickel five-cent piece (1866) helped increase the population of collectors. By 1867, a dealer estimated there were more than 3,000 people collecting coins in the United States.

Professional cataloging also began during this period of our industry's history. Dr. Edward Maris of Philadelphia was a pioneer in this area, having catalogued 39 varieties of the cents issued in 1794. He published his research into these cents in 1869, and the *American Journal of Numismatics* reviewed his pioneering effort, noting that from that day forward, the cents of 1794 would be known as "Maris I through Maris XXXIX."

Prior to the Centennial of the United States in 1876, the major interest of collectors was in colonial coins, early silver dollars, and medals of Washington, Lafayette and Franklin, among other colonial heroes and leaders. But the Centennial sparked a whole new crop of medals, and these began to be listed in the *American Journal of Numismatics*. Pieces were struck in every conceivable design and metal, as well as a popular set of "metals" that were formed by squeezing steamed black walnut pulp into the die.

More publications began to appear, and in 1877, Ed. Frossard published the first issue of *Numisma*, with particular attention being paid to the operations of the Philadelphia Mint, auctions and other offerings. For his efforts, Frossard became known as one of the first "watchdogs" of our industry.

While the private sale of coins from the Mint continued for some years afterward, it was no longer a guarded secret, and as early as 1879, the *American Journal of Numismatics* published a report that the 1878 patterns were distributed to members of Congress, but none were available to collectors. The *Journal*, in its condemnation of these actions, was careful to note that such machinations had stopped during "Mr. Lincoln's Administration," but had recommenced.

By 1885, the *New York Herald* newspaper reported that every major city in the nation had dealers who made a business of buying and selling coins, and that many journals were published to report on this subject. Grading was then, as now, a source of extensive public confusion, and the reporter who wrote the story could only maintain that the condition of the coin certainly was related in some way to its value. This demonstrates the lack of guidelines for grading and pricing in the first 70 years of our industry.

Collecting and selling continued apace through the remainder of the 19th Century, with such landmarks as the founding of the American Numismatic Association in 1891, and the establishment of *The Numismatist* (which became the ANA's monthly publication) in 1888. To give the reader a better idea of the relative size of the ANA at this time, the 1894 ANA national convention held in Detroit drew a crowd of 16 members!

During the last decade of the 19th Century, another current trend began: collecting coins according to mintmarks. By then, the Carson City (1879 to 1893), Charlotte (1835-1861), New Orleans (1838-1861 and 1879-1901), Philadelphia, Dahlonega, Ga. (1838-1861), and San Francisco (1854-1955, 1968 to Present) Mints had all produced sufficient quantities of coins to make each Mint a subject of collecting (the Denver Mint opened in 1906). Philadelphia was still the most popular Mint among collectors, since it produced the most coins in series, and its coins were easily found by collectors.

The value of individual coins increased as the Century turned, and by 1909, readers of *The Numismatist* were astonished to read that two coins had actually changed hands for $10,000 each! They were two unique $50 gold coins produced in 1877, and were regarded as the rarest coins in existance by collectors of that period (they were considered even rarer than the Brasher Doubloon). These coins were donated to the Smithsonian Institution in the same year, where they remain today.

In the late 19th Century (and ever since), collectors were clamoring for new designs and denominations of coins. Very few of the early patterns and designs were ever accepted and approved, or mass-produced as coinage. However, the Peace silver dollar design, that replaced the Morgan design silver dollar, is one rare example of a change in design that was originated by numismatists. Farran Zerbe proposed to the 1920 convention of the ANA that a new silver dollar design be minted to commemorate the end of The Great War (as it was then known). This proposal was accepted, and in 1921, the first Peace design silver dollars were minted, along with the Morgan issue. (The Morgan silver dollar was produced through 1921 and then ceased to be minted. The year 1921 was the only year that the Morgan design was produced at the Denver Mint).

Designed by Anthony DeFrancisci, the Peace dollar was acceptable in design, but not in form, to numismatists. The high relief made the coins difficult to stack (which also made them unacceptable to bankers, an error that was repeated in the 1970s when the Susan B. Anthony "silver" dollars were rejected due to difficulties of keeping them separated from the quarters in cash registers). This Peace design also led to excessive wear. As a result, the design was changed, and the relief was lowered, in the 1922 issue.

Interestingly enough, the value of the 1921 Peace dollars is higher than most of its successors in the series precisely because so few fully-struck coins have survived in Mint condition.

Other changes occurred in the 1920s as well, not the least of which was a dramatic shift in how coins were stored and displayed by collectors. Prior to this time, collectors had specially designed cabinets with many wooden shelves lined in velvet or other cloth in which to store their coins. Indeed, their collections were often referred to as "cabinets."

But in the 1920s, album pages and paper mounts began to be used to store and display the coins instead of the former wooden cabinets. This change led to the development of the excellent products available today for storing and preserving coins.

GLOSSARY

The process of converting large bars of pure silver and copper into finished Morgan and Peace silver dollars involved a series of steps and machinery. Since this process involved so many highly technical terms, and was a multi-phased operation, the following Glossary of terms relating to minting coins is intended to guide the reader through this technical chapter:

Annealing: This process involves heating the metal, and then allowing it to cool slowly in order to strengthen it. This process follows rolling of the metal into thin sheets.

Bagmarks: These are marks, abrasions or nicks caused by placing the newly-minted coins loosely into bags and then transporting those bags to their final destination.

Basining: A method of polishing the surface of a die used to mint coins.

Collar: A die used to produce the "reeding" on the rim of a coin.

Devices: The portraits and other designs on a coin, aside from the printed inscriptions and dates.

Dies: Metal forms used to stamp coins. Silver dollars were produced using die pairs and both obverse and reverse were stamped at the same time.

Die Cracks: Small imperfections in a coin produced due to cracks in the metal die used to mint the coins.

Frosted Surfaces: The white surface texture that is produced in the stamping process. When using new dies, this occurance is frequent.

Greasemarks: These slight imperfections in a coin are caused by lubrication of the die and this lubrication being struck into the metal of the coin's surface.

Hubs: Hubs are used to hold the pairs of dies in place in the press when coins are stamped. These hubs are cylinders of metal specially milled to serve this function.

Ingots: Large bars of metal used to produce coins. These ingots were rolled, stamped into planchets and milled prior to stamping into coins.

Milling: A process used to remove metal filings and clippings from planchets.

Mintmarks: These marks, located on the reverse of silver dollars, are the "signature" of the mint that produced the particular coin. These are: CC for Carson City; O for New Orleans; no mark for Philadelphia; D for Denver, and S for San Francisico.

Obverse: The front of a coin. There is the side on which the date appears.

Planchets: Metal blank discs in the circular shape of the finished coin that are stamped from sheets, milled to remove clippings and filings, annealed, and then fed into the press for stamping.

Presses: The U.S. Mints have used multiple types of presses: screw presses that require manual operation; steam presses which automated the stamping portion of the minting process; and pneumatic presses that are used to mint today's coins. Steam presses were used to produce the first Morgan dollar series.

Reeding: The vertical indentation around the rim of a silver dollar produced by a collar die during the stamping process.

Rolling: Rolling is the metallurgical technique of using heavy metal rollers to produce long, thin strips of metal from which planchets are stamped. The strips were repeatedly passed through rollers to produce the desired thickness of the coins.

Stamping: During stamping, the planchets received the impressions of the die pairs which produced the finished product, silver dollars.

Striking: This term describes the forcefulness of the impression that the dies cause in the planchets to produce silver dollars. Full strikes result in sharper impressions upon the finished coin. Lighter strikes result in less defined devices and inscriptions.

MINTING OPERATIONS

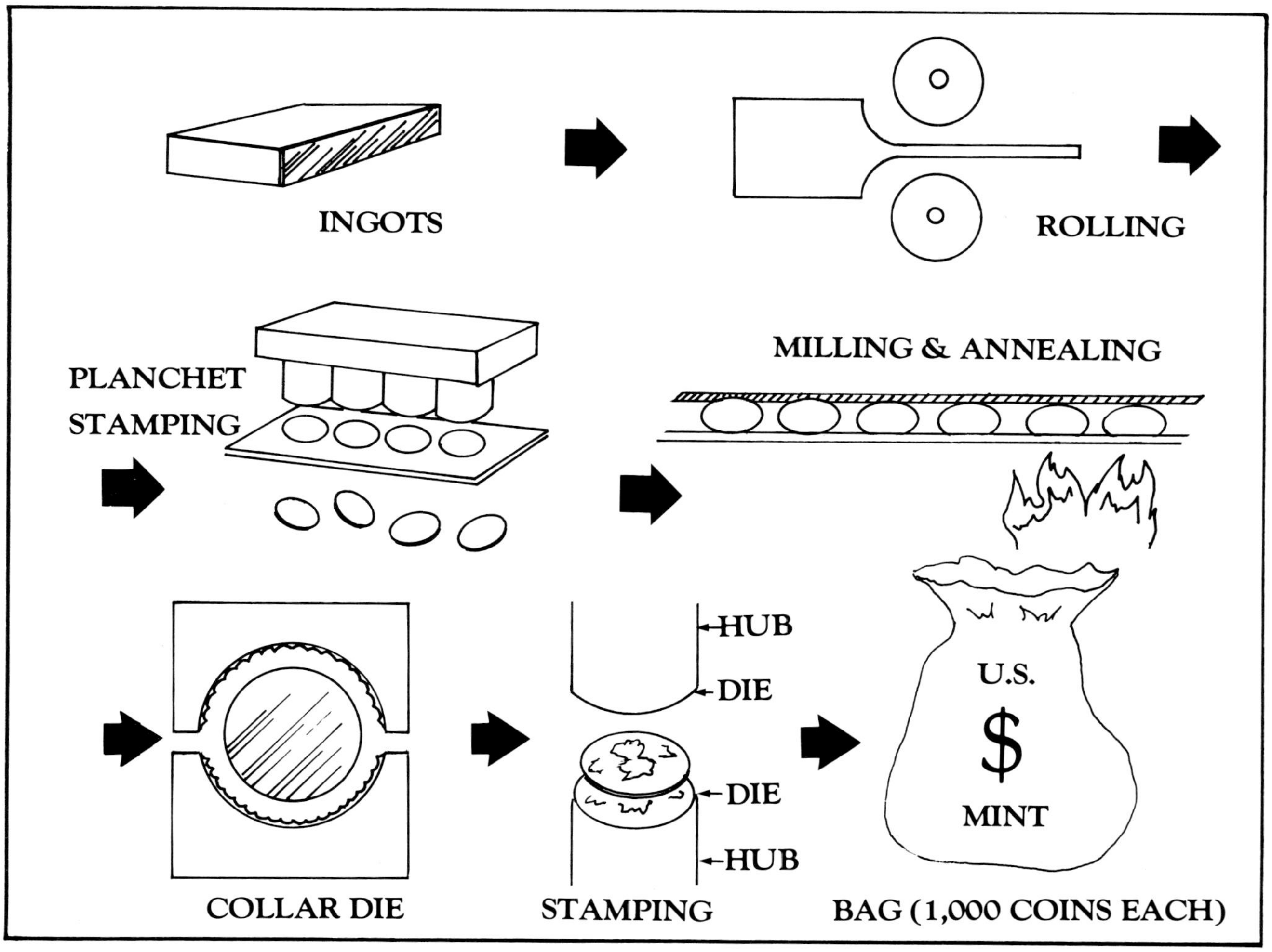

2

THE PROCESS OF MINTING COINS

Introduction:

After reviewing the Glossary of terms involved in the minting process, the reader gains a better concept of its complications. This process, remember, started in the 1790s, and required many intricate steps to insure the quality of the finished coins. The following is a simplified version of the process:

Essentially, ingots of raw metal were heated, rolled into thin strips, stamped into planchets (in much the same way that cookies are cut from a sheet), milled to remove filings and clippings, annealed to strengthen the planchets, and then stamped into coins.

This process of minting coins has an important effect upon some of the basic considerations that determine the coin's value to numismatists. The variations produced by the several Mints, as well as variations such as scratches, bagmarks, fullness of strike, greasemarks and luster, as well as other variables, are used to judge the value of an individual coin as well as the date minted. More details regarding Grading are provided in Chapter 4.

While the minting process can be described in a rather simple outline, as above, it is a complicated technical process of many steps. Each of these steps must be performed correctly and exactly in order to produce properly minted coins. In addition, several of these steps were quite labor-intensive (the screw type press is one example: it required from one to three men to stamp a single coin at a time, until these presses were replaced with steam presses).

Minting was also a very dangerous process for the Mint workers involved in some of the procedures. For example, the massive presses required considerable pressure to produce properly finished silver dollars (estimated at 150 tons per square inch). This tremendous force could result in personal injury if any of the machinery went awry. Much of the labor involved was unskilled labor and many practices of the Mint were based upon this fact.

Once the coins had been stamped, they were dropped into bags which contained 1,000 coins each when filled. These bags were then delivered to the various Federal Reserve depositories for distribution, or to the U.S. Treasury for storage. The resulting scratches and abrasions, not to mention nicks and gouges, are called "bagmarks." Bagmarks essentially detract from the beauty of the coin, and thereby reduce its relative value.

The surplus minted Morgan silver dollars which were not distributed were stored in bags at the Mint and in the U.S. Treasury Depositories. As will be more fully discussed in the chapter relating to the history of these coins, a large number were stored in the vaults and never destined for circulation. These totalled more than 300,000 coins by 1914. These coins have little or no wear, and therefore are of more value than circulated dollars of that era. However, more than 270,000 of these stored coins were remelted under the 1918 Pittman Act. This has also contributed to the higher value of uncirculated Morgan silver dollars.

By the time of the Peace silver dollar (1921 to 1928 and 1934-35), the entire operation of the Mints had been electrified and pneumatic coin presses installed. In addition, many of the Mint processes had also been altered. For one thing, the practice of basining the dies stopped, which resulted in an extremely rare chance of ever finding any prooflike Peace silver dollars. However, a few Peace dollars have slightly mirror-like surfaces which may be due to the process of stamping the coins with new die pairs. Peace dollars, while bagged in the same way, were at least not subjected to the same rough means of transportation as the Morgan series.

The following statistics describe finished silver dollars:

Total Weight: 26.73 grams (31.1 grams equals one Troy ounce)

Net Weight: .77344 Oz. pure silver

Composition: .900 silver, .100 copper

Diameter: 38.1 mm

The Coining Operation At the U.S. Mint in 1878:

At the time of the passage of the Bland-Allison Act in 1878, which created the Morgan design silver dollar, the U.S. Mint was not prepared to mint silver dollars immediately. In fact, the design had been officially adopted on the same day that the Act itself became law.

Dr. Henry Linderman, Director of the Bureau of the Mint from 1867-69 and 1873-78, and his staff put the pre-stamping operations into high gear immediately. Linderman instructed the Melter and Refiner to produce ingots at full speed using the entire work force available; the Coiner was instructed to receive the ingots and roll, cut, anneal, mill and clean planchets; and George T. Morgan, the designer of the new silver dollar, was told to hasten preparations of the hubs that would hold Engraver William Barber's pairs of dies during striking.

Linderman telegraphed these directions to his Philadelphia staff on the same day that the bill was enacted. (He was the first director of the Mint to have offices in Washington, D.C.). He had earlier reported in a letter to the Philadelphia superintendent, that he had selected the Morgan design for the new silver dollar. His decision was based on the low relief of the Morgan design, which required less power to bring up the devices and inscriptions on each coin.

By 1878, the Mint had been completely converted to steam power. The building that housed the earlier two-horse-team system had been destroyed by a fire in 1816, and the Mint had gradually replaced it, and the hand-operated minting equipment, with steam-powered, improved models. By the time of the Bland-Allison Act, the minting operation included steam-powered rolling, drawing and planchet-cutting machines. This equipment could produce more than 250 planchets a minute, which were then conveyed to the milling room.

After the planchets were milled to remove fillings (called shruff) and clippings, the reeded rim was placed on the still-blank planchets using a collar die. Finally, the reeded planchets were conveyed to the steam-powered coining press for stamping.

Built in 1874, by the Chief Coiner, this press was a vast improvement over its predecessor. One of the problems to be solved when using steam to power a coin press, compared with the hand-operated, screw-type presses that had preceeded it, was the frequency of weak strikes. The fast action of the steam press often resulted in poorly-struck coins. In 1874, however, the Coiner improved the stroke of the machine by redesigning it, and Morgan silver dollars were minted on this "Solid stroke" press beginning in 1878. This press created a better opportunity to produce fully-struck coins consistently.

The coining press utilized a pair of dies located at the end of hubs, or cyclinders, that impressed the top and bottom of the planchet at the same time. The minimum pressure required to produce the fully-struck Morgan devices and inscriptions is estimated at about 150 tons per square inch. Remember, these planchets were stamped cold, at least until the press and the dies themselves heated up through friction of operation. One of the reasons sometimes given for the generally softer striking of coins in the New Orleans series is the heat of the summer environment compared with more northern Mints.

After striking, the coins were dropped mechanically down a chute, then another planchet took its place in the dies, and the process was repeated many times a minute. This process resulted in a fairly large number of dies being damaged during a given year's production of silver dollars, which were large coins that strained the dies. The number of die pairs used ranged from about 10 sets to nearly 100 pairs of dies, and the number was directly related to the volume of coins produced, and the conditions at the individual Mints.

For example, in 1879, the Philadelphia Mint used 78 pairs of dies to produce nearly 15 million Morgan dollars; the Carson City Mint used 15 die pairs to produce 756,000 coins; the New Orleans Mint used 20 pairs of dies to mint almost 3 million Morgan dollars, and the San Francisco Mint produced more than 9 million Morgan silver dollars with 96 die pairs. The die pairs were replaced after cracks in the metal appeared, or if the pair was being worn smooth by the friction of the stamping process itself.

The reason that numismatists are concerned with statistics such as the number of die pairs used, is that it has a somewhat direct bearing on the number of very full strikes, as well as the number of prooflike pieces that the various mints produced in a single year. Proof coins are specially minted using polished metal surfaces. Very few were produced each year.

Fully-struck Morgan silver dollars had the best chance of being produced by a comparatively new die at full pressure. The die pairs were basined, a process that most often polished the fields more than the devices. These newly-polished dies are thought to have produced some of the "prooflike" coins in the Morgan series. These prooflike coins have a mirror-like finish, usually in the flat areas of the coin, while other Morgan dollars have what is called a "frosty" appearance on the devices. There are several types of prooflike coins, which vary according to whether or not both sides have mirror-like surfaces. All of these distinct characteristics are interesting to note since they were produced by the minting process itself. And they can certainly affect the selling price involved for these coins: many prooflike pieces are valued at multiples of the price for the same mintage and date in brilliant uncirculated grade.

It is important to note here that prooflike qualities have very little to do with grading of the coin using the Mint State system. The coin is whatever grade it merits based on the number of abrasions and other variables, including the strength of the impression of the dies on the planchet. A key factor to keep in mind is that prooflike coins appear to reflect more marks and abrasions due to the mirrored surfaces. This can result in a lowering of the grade of these coins.

Morgan Silver Dollar Variations: From the layman's point of view, all coins bearing the same year and mintmark might seem to be exactly the same. This is not always the case. Many years have multiple variations that appear in that year's production. Numerous examples of this occur throughout the Morgan series.

One illustration of this is found in coins minted during 1878 at Philadelphia. Although the observe of the coins remained constant for the entire year, the reverse involved three variations. These variations may seem slight, but these three coins are separated in value by several hundred dollars. One might expect these variations to be extremely noticeable, but in essence magnification is usually required to detect these minute differences. The chart (Appendix F) on page 197 shows the number of die varieties produced by the U.S. mint in each fiscal year.

Again, there are many years in the Morgan series that involve variations within one year's production. A thorough review of these distinctions is offered in Chapter 6.

Further Reading on Die Variations

Leroy Van Allen and A. George Mallis, *The Comprehensive Catalog and Encyclopedia of U.S. Morgan and Peace Silver Dollars.* New York: Arco Publishing Co. Inc., 1971.

Produced as a highly technical, exacting review of die varieties in Morgan and Peace series, this work is recommended for the reader who desires an extensive and *extremely thorough* research guide to microscopic variations between coins of the same date.

3

A BRIEF HISTORY OF SILVER DOLLARS MINTED IN THE UNITED STATES

Early Silver Dollars:

Even before the reverberations of the Battle of Yorktown faded, the infant United States was faced with the plethora of details required to run a separate nation effectively. Prior to the Revolutionary War, many of these details had been quietly handled at long range by King George III's appointees in London. One of these many and varied complications was the minting and distributing of money.

During the war itself, a popular phrase was "not worth a Continental," which reflects the level of the public's confidence in the early money of this nation. Indeed, the war was principally financed through the personal fortunes of the leaders of the Revolution such as Washington, Hancock, Jefferson, and others, because the Continental Congress did not have a continuing source of revenues. One of the basic causes of the Revolution was "Taxation without representation," and it didn't seem like an excellent idea to the Founding Fathers to begin levying taxes before they had achieved a satisfactory conclusion to the war.

After the war was won, and the new government organized along Federalist lines, it was time to begin considering the day-to-day business of running a new nation. Among the issues that had to be resolved was the creation of coinage.

President George Washington was among the ardent supporters of the idea that only the federal government should produce and distribute coinage. During the Revolutionary War, each state had been free to issue its own coinage. This led to some considerable problems for the populace. Under the Articles of Confederation, the form of government that preceeded the ratification of the Constitution, citizens often could not spend one state's money in another state. This was because each separate state reserved the right *not* to accept the other states' money as legal tender.

Washington and other early leaders decided this wasn't a very prudent way to run a country, at least from the monetary point of view. The earlier attempts at separate state coinages had resulted in a near halt to interstate commerce, for instance. One of the key tenets of the Federalists was that there were some functions that can be much better provided by the federal government than by state governments. One of these was the issuance of coinage.

In 1791, Congress had passed legislation enabling the creating of a federal mint. However, because of other, more urgent matters, no action was taken in that year. Nonetheless, President George Washington stressed the need for such action in his 1792 annual report to Congress, and the wheels of government began to turn slowly toward the issuance of coinage. In 1792, the Congress passed a specific bill mandating the issuance of copper cents and half-cents; gold eagles ($10), half-eagles and quarter-eagles, and silver dismes (later called "dimes"), dollars, half-dollars and quarter dollars.

The dollar and its decimal divisions had been approved as the basic unit of denomination as early as 1785, but no other action was taken until 1792, when the legislation described above was passed. This 1792 act also described the design of the money to be produced as

> . . . an impression or representation of the head of the President of the United States for the time being, with an inscription which shall express the initial or first letter of the Christian or first name and his surname at length, the succession of the presidency numerically, and the year of coinage; the reverse of the gold and silver coins to bear . . . an eagle with the inscription UNITED STATES OF AMERICA.

Washington didn't like the idea of his image being on the coinage, since it reminded him too much of the coinage produced by the monarchies of Europe. He preferred to have a symbol of Liberty placed on the front of each coin. His bust had appeared on Washington coins and tokens that were produced beginning in 1783, and perhaps these Colonial coins and tokens were the basis for his not wishing to be on the new nation's coinage.

In 1792, a lot for the site of the U.S. Mint was purchased in Philadelphia, and the new government began the issuance of coinage by private contract. In that same year, David Rittenhouse was named the first director of the U.S. Mint. An astronomer, philosopher and former Treasurer of the State of New Jersey, he laid the cornerstone for the first U.S. Mint Building in late July. By early September, the business of the Mint began in the new structure while construction was being completed. The first purchase of metal by the Mint occurred in mid-September with the purchase of six pounds of old copper, and the minting of coins began.

By the end of that year, President Washington was able to report to Congress that the minting of coinage had begun. However, due to a bonding difficulty (the amount was considered too high by the officials who were required by the enabling legislation to post bond), the coinage was not produced at the Mint itself, except for a small quantity of copper coins. Silver and gold coins were still produced outside the Mint. The original bond requirement was $10,000 each, later reduced to a total combined bond of $6,000 (both sums were considerable wealth at that time.)

Once the Mint officials, Albion Cox, Assayer, and Henry Voight, Chief Coiner, complied with this reduced bond requirement in 1794, minting of silver dollars began in the Mint building itself.

The design of the first silver dollar produced at the U.S. Mint in 1794 has been attributed to Robert Scot and is called the "flowing hair" type. It was produced during 1794 and 1795. The idea for the "Draped Bust" type silver dollar, first produced in 1795, was Gilbert Stuart's, an artist and celebrated portrait painter in Philadelphia at that time. Stuart had protested that the 1794 design was too "abandoned," and designed a new dollar with a more "matronly" appearance. As you may note, controversy about coinage began before the end of the first year of silver dollar minting in the United States.

The "Draped Bust" design was used until 1798 with a small eagle on the reverse. Early in that year, the reverse was redesigned to incorporate a larger, more impressive eagle. This was probably a reflection of the public spirit of the time.

Exactly 1,758 silver dollars were produced in 1794 at the Mint (all of these silver dollars were produced in a single day's work on October 15th). Approximately 100 examples of the 1794 silver dollar are said to remain in existance. In all, a total of about 1.5 million silver dollars were produced between 1794 and 1803. Interestingly enough, the 1794 and 1795 silver dollars included 15 stars on the obverse, not the 13 that traditionally represent the original 13 states, as on later coins.

The 1798 design continued to be minted until 1804. In that year, one of the first widespread controversies regarding U.S. coinage began. It appears that about 19,750 silver dollars were produced at the Mint during 1804, but the 1804-dated dollars in existance today were not among them. Apparently, the dollars minted in that year all bore earlier dates (1801, 1802 and 1803). Some reports indicate that the 1804 dollars were not actually minted until many years later, in 1834.

Thomas Jefferson halted the production of silver dollars in 1804 because of the "money-trading" activities of many citizens. It seems that the Spanish dollar, which was the value equivalent of the U.S. silver dollar, had slightly less silver in its content. As a result, silver U.S. dollars were traded in large quantities in the West Indies and Europe for slightly more than equal amounts of silver Spanish dollars. The Spanish dollars were then returned to the United States, where they were accepted as legal tender at face value. The difference between the number of U.S. silver dollars traded for Spanish dollars was apparently sufficient to make the effort required to trade them worthwhile.

When, in 1834, the State Department wished to send a presentation set of current U.S. coinage to the King of Siam, the government began minting the 1804 silver dollars which have caused such a stir among collectors and numismatists ever since. The 1804 silver dollars produced in 1834, and as late as 1840, have probably been the source of more stories, gossip and reportage than any other coins in U.S. history.

In 1836, Christian Gorbrecht was hired as assistant to Mint engraver William Kneass, and he designed a number of pattern coins for silver dollars (patterns are artists' designs that were not accepted by the government for actual coinage). These designed were based on drawings by Thomas Sully and Titian Peale, and bore Gorbrecht's name as well as a seated image of Liberty on the obverse. The reverse bore an image of an eagle in flight amid 26 stars and the words "United States of America." Due to public criticism, Gorbrecht's name was removed from the obverse in 1838. This is the first time a dollar was named after its designer, and these coins are still referred to as "Gorbrecht dollars."

The Seated Liberty design was produced from 1840 to 1873. About 6.6 million pieces were struck during that period. Also during this 34-year series, dollars minted in San Francisco, Carson City, and New Orleans began to appear as these branch Mints opened.

Minting of silver dollars again stopped in 1873, this time because of debates about whether silver or gold should be the standard for coinage in the United States. Congress passed legislation that firmly placed the nation on the gold standard, but also approved enabling legislation for a

U.S. Trade silver dollar. This was meant for use in the very active China trade, but Congress also accidently made the Trade dollar legal tender in the United States. This error was corrected in 1874, and about 367 million Trade dollars were produced between 1873 and 1878, when the Morgan design began to be produced. However, proofs of the Trade dollar were produced until 1885.

In 1878, Congress reversed itself on the issue of the use of silver as legal tender due to silver mining industry lobbying efforts. The uneasy economy of the 1870s has been attributed by some to Congressional debates about the use of both gold and silver as legal tender, and many heated arguments occurred in Congress regarding this topic in that troubled decade. In fact, remnants of this argument remain in our country to this day.

However, in February 1878, Congress passed the Bland-Allison Act, which restored the silver dollar's status as legal tender in the United States. The act required that the U.S. Treasury purchase between $2 million and $4 million worth of silver each month in order to produce silver dollars. This had the effect of restoring the health of the silver mining industry in the United States, as well as restoring public confidence in other U.S. silver coinage.

The Morgan Silver Dollar:

The Morgan silver dollar was designed by George T. Morgan using Anna Williams, a 19-year-old school teacher in Philadelphia at the time, as the model. The reverse bore the design of an eagle with wings outspread surrounded by a wreath.

Morgan came to the U.S. Mint for the temporary project in 1876. He had served under Wyon at the Royal Mint in London for a number of years, and had attended the South Kensington Art School. Mint Director Henry Linderman employed Morgan as an assistant to William and Charles Barber for six months, but it turned out that Morgan stayed at the Mint for a total of 48 years instead.

Vast quantities of Morgan design silver dollars were produced between 1878 and 1880. In fact, more than 22 million were produced in 1878 alone at the Philadelphia, Carson City and San Francisco Mints. Perhaps this was an effort to appease the silver standard faction in the nation, as well as restore the health of the country's economy. In 1879, New Orleans also began to produce Morgan silver dollars, and a total of more than 40 million were produced at the four mints in that year.

In all, more than 378 million Morgan silver dollars were produced under the Bland-Allison Act, and an additional 187 million were produced under the Sherman Silver Purchase Act of 1890, which repealed the Bland-Allison Act. The 1890 legislation was a blatant subsidy of the silver mining industry in the United States, and allowed the U.S. Treasury to purchase as much as 4.5 million ounces of silver each month with bonds. These bonds were redeemable in either the new silver dollars that the act provided for, or in gold. This satisfied both camps of the silver vs. gold standard argument, but not for long. In 1893, the Sherman Act itself was also repealled due to the efforts of President Grover Cleveland. It seems the Sherman Act had further worsened the gold drain from the U.S. Treasury that had begun much earlier. Silver dollar production remained low under Cleveland's Administration, which ended in 1896.

In 1898, yet another coinage law was passed in Congress which called for all of the available silver bullion then stored in the Treasury to be minted into silver dollars. This supply lasted until 1904, when silver dollar production again ceased. By then, more than 570 million Morgan silver dollars had been minted.

This huge quantity of silver dollars was sufficient to cause Congress to take steps to drastically reduce the supply of them. No new silver dollars were produced between 1905 and 1920, and there was still a tremendous glut of them in evidence. There was no silver bullion in the government's vaults, but there were plenty of Morgan silver dollars, so the Congress passed the Pittman Act of 1918, which allowed the government to melt as many as 350 million of the existing silver dollars and return them to a bullion state. This bullion could then be used to produce smaller denomination coins for general distribution.

Between 1918 and 1920, a total of more than 270 million Morgan silver dollars was converted to bullion and reminted into other denominations of coins, or just sold outright as bullion. Indeed, most of the bullion went to England, and only about 11 million silver coins were ever produced from this supply of bullion.

As must be obvious by now, silver dollars were a subject of considerable controversy in the Congress, and reversals of its position were very frequent. In spite of the fact that Congress had approved the melting down of hundreds of millions of silver dollars in 1918, it had reversed itself again by 1921, and a total of 86 million additional Morgan silver dollars were minted in that year. By the time the U.S. Mints ceased production of Morgan silver dollars in 1921, a total of more than 657 million had been produced over a span of six decades.

The Peace Silver Dollar:

In 1920, one of the few examples of the government paying any heed to suggestions from numismatists occurred.

At the 1920 convention of the American Numismatic Association, Farran Zerbe voiced a popular sentiment that the Mint should issue a new silver dollar design to commemorate the end of The Great War. What later came to be known as the First World War had been a tremendous drain on the nation, both economically and emotionally. An entire generation of Europeans, Americans and Australians had been literally decimated in the prolonged conflict, and the populace was greatly relieved by the Versailles peace agreements reached in 1918. Congress finally approved the concept in 1921, and a design competition was held for the new silver dollar.

A design by Anthony DeFrancisci was selected for the new Peace dollar. Some sources believe there was political motivation involved in the selection since more famous designers such as Victor D. Brenner and Henry Hering competed, but their designs were not chosen. Nonetheless, DeFrancisci's design based on the portrait of his 21-year-old wife, Teresa, was chosen for the obverse of the new Peace Dollars. It has been argued that the new, more powerful design was selected because it suited the mood of the nation, and the hope that Peace would last forever. The reverse featured an eagle, perched and alert, with an olive branch in its talons.

Production of the new Peace dollars began in 1921, and immediately resulted in difficulties, both from bankers and from the numismatists who had so strongly supported the Peace design concept. It seems that the new design was initially produced with a very high relief (this means that the coin was much thicker in some areas on the obverse and reverse than the Morgan design dollars). This relief made the coins extremely difficult to stack, which irritated the bankers; and high relief contributed to very rapid wear, which didn't make the coin collectors or the numismatists very happy either.

George Morgan was by now the Chief Engraver at the Philadelphia Mint, and in 1922 he revised the design with a lower profile that satisfied these objections. While the new lower relief wore better, it is usually not as highly valued by numismatists as the 1921 higher relief Peace dollars. This is for precisely the ironic reason that fewer high quality pieces remain from the December 1921 production of about 1 million Peace design coins. The only 1922 Peace dollars struck with the 1921 high relief are the rare matte proofs.

The Peace dollar was produced from 1921 to 1928, when the ceiling of 270 million coins imposed by Congress in the enabling legislation was reached. Since no further legislation was passed, no Peace silver dollars were produced until Franklin D. Roosevelt approved a proclamation in December 1933 which enabled the Mints to issue slightly more than 7 million Peace dollars in 1934. He extended this permision into 1935, and about 53,000 dollars of this design were minted in that year.

No further Peace design dollars were produced until 1964, and here another extremely major controversy in the history of U.S. silver dollars arises. It seems that Congress approved the production of 45 million silver dollars in that year, and the U.S. Mint dusted off the old Peace design and produced a total of just over 316,000 silver dollars, dated 1964. The Denver Mint produced these dollars, but plans for the distribution of the silver dollars were never realized. The controversy stems from the variance of opinions regarding whether or not *all* of these coins were melted down as ordered by the Director of the Mint.

Later "Silver" Dollars:
The Peace silver dollars marked the end of what I consider the true silver dollar era. From 1840 through the Peace series (including Trade dollars), the silver content of dollars was .900 silver and .100 copper. Beginning with the Eisenhower dollar series, first produced in 1971 to commemorate the Apollo landing on the Moon and to honor the former President, much less silver was used in minting dollars. These dollars were issued in nickel-copper, rather than .900 silver and .100 copper. Some silver *clad* pieces were produced from 1971 through 1974 and in 1976, however. For this reason, the later issues of dollar denomination coins are not favored by numismatists and are rarely referred to as "silver" dollars at all.

The Eisenhower-design featured a portrait of the former President on the obverse, and a modified logo of the Apollo Moon Mission on the reverse. This reverse design showed an eagle with wings outspread landing on the Moon with the Earth in the background. The reverse design was changed in 1976 to commemorate the BiCentennial. A total of about 617 million one dollar coins were produced in the Eisenhower and BiCentennial series.

The Susan B. Anthony dollars produced beginning in 1979 is another example of extremely unpopular coinage. Numismatists *never* refer to these pieces as "silver" dollars either, and for the same reasons as the Eisenhower series: they were minted in outer layers of copper and nickel

(.750 copper, .250 nickel) over a core of pure copper.

Aside from the debased metal used for their production, these coins were a functional disaster. They were only about as big as a quarter, and they were extremely unpopular as a result, since they didn't "seem" to be worth a dollar, especially compared to earlier series.

In addition, they were constantly being confused with quarters in cash registers. This made them very unfavorable to bankers and retailers, as well as business in general. Having both the business community and the general populace against them, the Mints ceased production of these coins in 1981, and they were recalled. A total of about 800 million of these unsuccessful coins were produced in their three-year lifetime.

Summary: From a numismatist's point of view, the very early silver dollars, including the Flowing Hair, Draped Bust, Seated Liberty, Trade, Morgan and Peace dollars are all very favorable pieces. However, due to their rarity and the resulting prices they command, silver dollars minted before the Morgan series (which began in 1878) have limited feasibility as investments in high quality, at least for investors just beginning their involvement with silver dollars.

I usually recommend that initial investments be made in selected years, dates and mintages of the Morgan and Peace series, since these are the most populated and the most actively traded. These series are the most attractive for the new investor, based on the successful investment strategy I will outline in Chapter 7, for that reason, Chapter 6, which lists the total production and a variety of statistics about each silver dollar produced at the various Mints over the years, is limited to the Morgan and Peace series.

4

THE MINT STATE GRADING SYSTEM

When considering the topic of grading, it is necessary to make a very important initial distinction: the difference between grading and pricing. Many beginning investors believe that these two topics are one and the same, but this is not true. The definition of these terms helps to relieve this misconception.

Grading is the process of individually evaluating a particular coin relative to its original Mint State condition; that is, how closely it matches the ideal state of a coin when originally produced at the Mint. This evaluation is based on a variety of factors, including: 1) the relative state of the coin in terms of bagmarks, abrasions, scratches and nicks; 2) the original luster, and how much of that luster remains; 3) the "toning" or coloration of the coin (it is perfectly natural for coins to tone over the years and, in most cases, adds to, rather than detracts from, the value); 4) the fullness of the strike; 5) the number of variations in dies involved in that year's production; and 6) unusual conditions such as striations or greasemarks that are stamped into the coin's surface.

On the other hand, pricing is a combination of the Mint State grade of a given coin, along with other considerations such as the number of coins available in that grade from that Mint and year; the demand in the marketplace for that coin in a particular grade (some coins have been unavailable for many years — this increases the demand involved in that coin's price); and the buyer's and seller's estimates of the potential return on investment for that coin.

In addition, pricing also involves other factors such as the need to liquidate a collection or portfolio for a gamut of reasons. These "extra-market" considerations include divorce, bankruptcy, death of the owner, taxes, a desire to use the portfolio's value for another purpose, dissolution of a partnership, or other needs to convert the tangible assets of coins into immediate liquid capital. Yet another factor is the economy's relative health in general. Obviously, when the economy is experiencing difficulties, these spread to most kinds of businesses, sometimes including numismatists. When this happens, companies may feel a need to liquidate some of their own portfolio as well.

With this distinction firmly in mind, it is possible to proceed to a more thorough discussion of grading.

Historical Grading:

In the early days of numismatics, pricing was based almost exclusively on considerations of "what the market would bear." This was reasonable because the industry involved a handful of dealers and several hundred collectors in total.

However, the temptation to exaggerate the value of coins is almost as old as the profession itself, and problems began soon after the first organized sales relating to descriptions of coins. For some coins, this was rectified by standardizing grading, as was the case with the 1794 large copper cents which were categorized in the 39-step Maris grading system. This system identified 39 variations in the 1794 production of large cents, and this aided in standardizing grading of these particular coins.

For much of the history of numismatics, descriptive adjectives have been used to grade coins. This would work well, *if* everyone used the same descriptions for the same characteristics. Unfortunately, this was and is not the case: discrepancies and variations led to considerable confusion and naturally to suspicion of grading in general among collectors and investors.

Some numismatists still use a form of descriptive adjectives for grading, and the American Numismatic Association system of grading is a combination of this system with a Mint State grading system for uncirculated coins. This is the most common combination in use today. Later in this discussion, I will propose a significant refinement to this system, which, I believe, will further standardize grading, especially for silver dollars.

The Mint State Grading System.

The Mint State grading system was originally developed by Dr. William H. Sheldon in relation to grading cents, and first published in his book *Penny Whimsy* in 1958. This system used a scale of 1 to 70, with 70 being the perfect, and exact, Mint State, and 1 being the most worn known coin.

This system added greatly to standardizing grading when its application was expanded to include all other United States coins, as well as cents. Grading is divided into two major categories: Circulated coins and Uncirculated coins. The key distinction in initially evaluating a coin is whether or not it was used in public circulation.

Since there are obviously a much smaller number of uncirculated coins than circulated coins (especially after the Pittman Act resulted in the melting of millions of uncirculated silver dollars), the uncirculated coins are graded at the higher end of the Mint State scale. Uncirculated coins begin at Mint State 60, and coins at lower grades are referred to as Mint State 1 to 59.

The Mint State system was further refined in 1970 and officially established as the grading system for the A.N.A., as defined in *A.N.A. Grading Standards For United States Coins*, published in that year.

The Mint State grading system as adopted by the A.N.A. includes: (lowest to highest)

Circulated Coins:

AG-3	About Good
G-4	Good
VG-8	Very Good
F-12	Fine
VF-30	Very Fine
EF-40	Extremely Fine
EF-45	Choice Extremely Fine
AU-50	About Uncirculated
AU-55	Choice About Uncirculated
MS-60	Uncirculated
MS-65	Choice Uncirculated
MS-70	Perfect Uncirculated

Further Refinements Inherent In The Mint State System:

In the dozen or so years since this system was officially adopted as the A.N.A. grading system, a number of refinements have been added. These include MS-63 (halfway between MS-60 and MS-65), MS-67 (halfway between MS-65 and MS-69) and MS-69 (this is due to the extreme rarity of MS-70 perfect coins. In more than 15 years of collecting, this author has never seen an MS-70, business strike, silver dollar.)

The MS-64 grade, which has not been previously used for grading, is a further capability of the Mint State system. A large number of silver dollars exist which in past years have been graded MS-63, or MS-65, incorrectly. For that reason, I propose to use the MS-64 grade in this chapter's review of silver dollar grades.

There are a number of instances in which the MS-64 grading is the most appropriate grade, a few of which I will now outline:

First, there are a large number of silver dollars that are higher quality coins than those normally found in average uncirculated rolls of coins. These "average" rolls are usually considered to be composed of MS-63 silver dollars. Many of these same pieces, while of higher quality than MS-63, at the same time do not have all of the characteristics of an MS-65 silver dollar. For that reason, I would classify these coins as true examples of the MS-64 grade.

Another example is a silver dollar that has MS-64 characteristics on one side, and MS-65 characteristics on the other. As a normal business practice, these coins should be graded MS-64, simply because the rule of thumb in our industry is to grade a "split-grade" coin at the lower of the two grades. Grading this coin at MS-65 would be a disservice to all parties, as would grading it an MS-63.

A third instance of an MS-64 grade coin is a coin that would normally grade as an MS-65, except that one side is less fully struck than the other. This is usually due to a difference in the age and wear of the obverse and reverse dies; one may be much newer than the other in some cases. Obviously, it would be unfair to grade this type of coin at MS-63, but equally inappropriate to grade it at full MS-65 grade.

A fourth case of an MS-64 grade is a coin that in all specifications meets the MS-65 characteristics, *except* that it might have a large bagmark in an obvious location such as the cheek of a Morgan dollar, or the field of a Peace dollar. Using the same logic as in the previous three examples, it would be inequitable to grade this coin as either an MS-63 or an MS-65, making it a true MS-64 silver dollar as well.

Again, I believe it is our professional responsibility as numismatists to acknowledge the large population of coins that truely fall into the MS-64 grade; to begin grading those coins at their true level, and to price these coins appropriately. In the past, many part time dealers, or unscrupulous mail order houses would attempt to sell these coins at MS-65, but I believe that attempt does both the individual investor, and our industry as a whole, an extreme disservice.

For those reasons, this chapter will provide characteristics and examples for the MS-64 grade for both Morgan and Peace silver dollars.

By correctly using the Mint State system, I realize that I am open to criticism for further "complicating" the Mint State system. However, exactly the opposite is the intention of this proposal.

I believe that all of the even numbers between MS-60 and MS-70 will eventually be used to grade coins, and for the same reasons that I am currently proposing the use of the MS-64 grade: the coins themselves justify this usage; and the exactness which is *possible* in the Mint State system (but not now being employed fully) will greatly aid in standardizing our industry's grading, as is demanded by today's investors.

Proof-Like Grades:

As noted in the previous chapters, there are many types and qualities of proof-like silver dollars. Remember, these coins are produced by new or newly-polished die pairs, resulting in shiny, mirror-like surfaces. All of the proof-like silver dollars are in uncirculated condition, but they vary widely in terms of bagmarks, nicks and abrasions.*

---

*Proof-like coins are *extremely* rare in the Peace series; therefore proof-like grades (MS-63 and MS-65) are listed for Morgan silver dollars only.

AG-3
ABOUT GOOD

MORGAN

The obverse of AG-3 Morgan dollars retain the complete outline of the head, but almost all of the details have been removed by wear. Most areas of the design will be very weakly visible, and the date is worn, but readable. The legend on these coins tends to fade into the rim area, a complete rim surrounding the coin will not show. The reverse has the same characteristic of the legend fading into the rim, and near total wear on the designs.

PEACE

As in the Morgan dollar, the head on the obverse of this grade of Peace dollar shows only the outline, with very little detail remaining. In addition, areas of the date and inscription may be worn away. The inscription fades into the rim and the date is still readable in spite of the excessive amount of wear. The reverse has the same characteristics of outlined devices and inscriptions fading into the rim. The Peace label under the eagle is barely legible.

G-4
GOOD

MORGAN

The obverse has a full date, letters and design clearly outlined, but the hair is well worn. In spite of wear, the rim is complete all the way around the coin (obverse and reverse). The reverse will show a complete outline on the eagle, but the remainder of the eagle is worn nearly flat. The inscription should all be legible.

PEACE

The obverse has clear, full date, inscription and design outlines, but is well worn. Letters of the inscription tend to fade into the rim in some locations, and very little detail remains on the devices. The reverse eagle design shows the outline of the eagle, but is worn flat in many places. The inscription fades into the rim in some places.

VG-8
VERY GOOD

MORGAN

The obverse letters and date are clear, but most of the details from the hair, cotton blossoms and leaves are flat. The reverse eagle design is worn on both wings, with the left-hand wing nearly flat, as are the leaves in the wreath. Both front and back rims are complete in this grade.

PEACE

The hair on the obverse is worn, and the rays will have some very weak detail. While the rim should be complete in this grade, the inscription may be weak in places. The reverse eagle has worn spots on the right leg and wing, as well as on the neck and head. Parts of the inscriptions are missing. Rims on front and back are complete in this grade.

F-12
FINE

MORGAN

The entire design should be clear on both obverse and reverse in this grade, in spite of moderate to heavy wear. The obverse design features a sharp hairline along the face, while the two cotton blossoms at bottom are worn, but have a distinct outline from the cap. Two lines should show in each cotton blossom, in spite of wear. The reverse eagle device has slightly worn tail feathers, with flat areas on the right wing and edge of the left wing. The top leaves on the wreath will show heavy wear in this grade.

PEACE

In this grade the obverse design has smooth hair areas around the face and some signs of wear on the bun and back of the neck. The rays show wear as well. The reverse eagle's feathers are worn on the right leg, and only the lowest horizontal line of the feather layers will remain. While readable, the devices are usually worn partially away in this grade.

VF-30
VERY FINE

MORGAN

The obverse in Very Fine grade features smooth areas in the hair above the ear and heavily worn, but distinguishable, cotton leaves. The wheat grains also show wear in this grade. The reverse eagle has a smooth breast and weak wing tips, though the lines are complete. Only a few feathers will show on the head in this grade.

PEACE

The obverse shows light to moderate even wear with weak details in the hair around the face and light wear on the upper wave of hair. Single strands should be defined above the ear. The reverse eagle has weak feather detailing on the right wing and the leg and neck features also show signs of wear. The motto also shows signs of wear.

EF-45
EXTREMELY FINE

MORGAN

The obverse shows very light wear in areas such as the hair above the date, the forehead and the ear. Hair lines should be well defined and sharp, though very small signs of wear show on the cheek areas. There are flat spots at the tips of the cotton leaves. Both obverse and reverse have some original luster. The reverse design has lightly-worn breast feathers on the eagle and wear on the tops of the legs and the right wing tip.

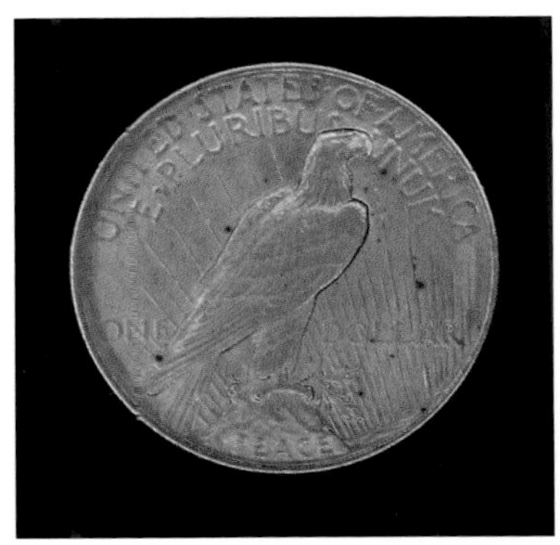

PEACE

Very light wear on the highest points is also characteristic of Peace dollars in this grade. On the obverse this shows in the hair around the face, and the lower edge of the neck. On the reverse, the wear shows at the top of the neck and the head behind the eye, as well as the central wing and leg feathers. In this grade, about half of the original mint luster should be apparent.

**AU-55
ABOUT
UNCIRCULATED**

MORGAN

In AU-55, small amounts of wear are visible, and only on the highest areas. On the obverse these are on the hair above the ear and eye, on the edges of the cotton leaves, and the upper fold of the cap. Most original luster should be visible on the cheek. The reverse areas of slight wear are in the breast area, legs and talons of the eagle device.

PEACE

The obverse shows traces wear on the hair above the ear and the forehead and some light wear on the cheek. The reverse eagle wear is on the high areas of the right wing. Most original luster should be evident.

MS-60 UNCIRCULATED

MORGAN

The key distinction between this grade and those preceeding it, is circulation. A coin is either circulated or uncirculated. The MS-60 coin has no wear, but does show considerable bagmarks and abrasions, as well as a few possible small rim nicks. These coins also have full mint luster, though it may be dulled, and surfaces may be heavily toned or spotted.

PEACE

These absolutely uncirculated coins have no trace of wear either, though they may exhibit considerable bagmarks and abrasions and possibly a few rim nicks. These coins may also be weakly struck and have full mint luster, though dulled, as above. In addition, the surfaces may be heavily spotted or toned.

MS-63
CHOICE
UNCIRCULATED

MORGAN

In both the Morgan and Peace series, and MS-63 coin is one that has retained its mint luster, but has obvious bagmarks, nicks or abrasions which detract from its overall beauty. When referring to silver dollars, this grade is ideally what average rolls of uncirculated dollars should grade.

PEACE

As noted above, the MS-63 has obvious marks which distinguish it from other, higher grades of uncirculated silver dollars. Both obverse and reverse should also have original mint luster. When referring to silver dollars, this grade is ideally what average rolls of uncirculated dollars should grade.

MS-64
NEARLY GEM
UNCIRCULATED

MORGAN

As noted in the introduction, the MS-64 grade is commonly a "between" grade which is composed, in the Morgan series, in many cases, of coins which have one side that would grade better than MS-63 and the other side MS-65. Other examples include a coin which is less sharply struck on one side than the other, due to the age and wear of the dies. There are a large number of coins that are better than MS-63 roll material, but do not grade as MS-65 singles.

PEACE

A number of the Peace MS-64 dollars seen by this author are of the type also described in the Introduction, which would grade at MS-65 except for a large nick or abrasion on the obverse or reverse, which would reduce the grade to MS-64, not to MS-63. There are a large number of coins that are better than MS-63 roll material, but do not grade as MS-65 singles.

MS-65
GEM
UNCIRCULATED

MORGAN

The key distinctions between MS-65 coins and lower MS grades is the brilliance of the original mint luster, and the smaller and fewer bagmarks and abrasions. There should be no wear on these coins whatsoever, as with all other Mint State uncirculated grades. They should be sharply struck.

PEACE

MS-65 Peace dollars also have no signs of any wear and retain full Mint luster and brilliance. They should be sharply struck (though Peace dollars are usually less fully struck in this grade than Morgan dollars), and may be unevenly toned.

MS-67
SUPERB GEM
UNCIRCULATED

MORGAN

This uncirculated coin should have original mint luster and be close to flawless, be 100 percent fully struck, virtually approaching perfection with the exception of very minor nicks or imperfections. Even then, these nicks must be very few in number, and not in major areas of the coin such as Liberty's face or eagle devices.

PEACE

The Peace series has the same general characteristics as the Morgan dollar series in Mint State 67; 100 percent full strike, original Mint luster, virtually approaching perfection. Any minute bagmarks or nicks must be few in number and not in prominent major areas of the coin such as the face or eagle devices.

MS-69
NEAR PERFECT*

MORGAN

These coins are as nearly perfect as it is possible to obtain: they should have full mint luster and brilliance, be *fully struck* and have *absolutely no* signs of wear. *Extremely minute* surface mars such as a striation or a tiny bag mark differentiate these coins from perfect MS-70 coins. Any unusual striking characteristics should be fully described, as should any unusual toning of the coins.

PEACE

Again these coins are very close to perfect in every possible way. Only one or two minute abrasions or bag marks differentiate them from a perfect coin. Unusual striking should be fully described.

* As with any man-made product, these coins show some *very minor* imperfections.

MS-63
PROOFLIKES

These choice, uncirculated dollars have the same characteristics as MS-63 coins except for the addition of mirror, prooflike surfaces on both obverse and reverse.

MS-65
PROOFLIKES

These gem uncirculated dollars have exactly the same characteristics as MS-65 coins, with the addition of deep mirror, prooflike surfaces on both obverse and reverse.

5

TODAY'S INVESTOR IN SILVER DOLLARS

Professional numismatists are often asked why the field of silver dollar investing has increased so much in popularity in recent years.

Depending upon who is asked, the answers vary widely; however, one underlying theme reoccurs in most: the present economy places particular value on *any* investment which has an historically established record of continuing appreciation.

Part of this emphasis is due to the widely fluctuating values of most other investments: stocks have fluctuated widely over the past decade with large gains possible, but with large losses possible as well; bullion has swung from more than $800 an ounce for gold in 1980 to about $400 an ounce in 1982, with wide swings within that range during the same period; art has experienced skyrocketing increases and devastating crashes; real estate has suffered from high interest rates; the dollar has suffered from oil import trade volume deficits. No matter what the medium, problems have surfaced in recent years which have clouded the "glow," in terms of potential investors.

Silver dollars, on the other hand, have continued to increase in value in the "stair-step" pattern I have already referred to, in spite of interest rates, bullion prices, the overall health of the world economy. Silver dollars have even outdistanced all other forms of collectibles investments.

So, return on investment is a major source of the increased popularity of silver dollar investing; however, it is not the only reason for this gain in investment activity. Other reasons include the more favorable taxation that silver dollars offer; the versatility of the silver dollar investment, and the potential for a wide range of uses for the silver dolars themselves, from use as a trade medium, to tax benefits. Another major factor on silver dollar investing is the economy. In spite of the fact that economic factors have not *adversely* affected silver dollar investing over the decades, there *has* been a very strong *positive* impact from economic shifts and conditions. Whenever the economy has declined signficantly, as in the early 1970s and early 1980s, interest in silver dollar investing has increased proportionately.

In other words, when short-term economic news is bad, the effect on long-term investments such as silver dollars is good. Again, this is particularly the case for silver dollars due to their unequalled track record.

In terms of the taxes paid after the silver dollar portfolio, or parts of it has reached maturity, and is sold, this income is taxed at the more favorable capital gains rate (a maximum of 20 percent), if the portfolio is owned for at least one year. At the same time, tax benefits can also be developed by donating all, or portions, of the silver dollar portfolio to a non-profit institution. Naturally, the Federal tax laws list some very specific restrictions on this activity, both for the donor and the recipient institution, but in many cases significant tax benefits can result.

Major Types of Silver Dollar Investors:

There are several major "types" of silver dollar investors that have been entering this investment field in increasing numbers in recent years. These include individuals; investment groups and clubs; corporations, and institutions of various kinds.

Individuals can benefit from investments in silver dollars, not only in terms of income and profit development, but also in terms of tax benefits, estate planning, and the transference of family wealth from one generation to the next. Since rare silver dollars have averaged a 20+ percent increase in value each year for decades, the income and profit potential of these investments is obvious. As stated above, this return is *unparalleled* over the long term by any other form of investment.

Tax benefits have already been discussed briefly, and the best way to determine if silver dollars can be of benefit to you personally is to arrange for an individual appointment with a professional numismatist and your accountant. These experts can examine your situation, your investment portfolio, and other personal finance variables to determine the best way to tailor fit a silver dollar portfolio for your exact needs. Generally, however, it is permissable for an individual to donate up to 30 percent of his or her *bottom-line* taxable income each year (U.S. Tax Code, Section 170). This means that it is possible to donate nearly one-third of your taxable income (the figure at the bottom of the tax return), and thereby reduce that year's tax obligation apportionately.

Transferring family wealth is another advantage of silver dollars. Since they are easy to store and a sound long-term investment, many people give them to their children and grandchildren for special events such as birthdays, Christmas, etc. The tax laws allow each family member to give each child up to $3,000 per year in whatever form they may wish. This means that it is possible to give a younger family member (though it could just as easily be an older family member under the law) silver dollars amounting to $3,000 each per year, without paying taxes on that gift.

In addition, many people use silver dollars as an informal type of retirement program. In this way, a person can purchase silver dollars gradually over a period of years, and not pay taxes on the value of the silver dollars until they are sold. Once again, the proceeds are taxable at capital gains rates, rather than personal income tax rates, a very favorable difference. Many people have gradually built up a considerable retirement investment fund in this way in recent decades, which can then be reinvested to provide retirement income, used to purchase property for retirement, or any other function desired.

Groups and investment clubs also have been investing in gem quality silver dollars for a number of years. The typical organization of these groups is a pooled fund of resources which is invested at the consensus of the group's participants in a particular investment product or products. The group also typically sets investment goals, most often in terms of optimum return on investment; the desired term of the investment;

how profits will be divided, and other operational details.

Once the group's funds are invested, each participant in the group can be as active in monitoring its progress as he or she wishes. Many groups schedule regular meetings (monthly, quarterly, annually, depending on the form and term of the investment) to discuss and monitor their investments.

There are thousands of investment clubs and groups actively involved in silver dollar investing, and a potential member may either start a new group, or locate an existing investment group or club in his or her community through available listings. In addition, several national organizations exist that will provide outlines of investment club organization and establishment, guidelines for decision-making, and recommendations for individual investments.

Corporations and organizations of other similar kinds (partnerships, for example) have also become more active in recent years in the field of silver dollar investing. Corporations have several viable options when considering silver dollar investments; the most popular of which are profit generation, and executive incentive programs, or "perks". Naturally, corporations often invest in silver dollar portfolios for income production, just as many individuals and groups do. However, executive incentive programs are a fairly new wrinkle in the silver dollar investment field.

"Perks" are a natural area of silver dollar activity because they offer the same tax advantages to the individual that any other silver dollar investment does, as well as offer a perquisite or executive bonus which continues to increase in value the longer they are held. While restrictions have tightened on executive perks such as stock options in recent years, all of the same benefits and requirements apply to the executive benefit programs involving silver dollars as to individual investments: these silver dollars may be held for appreciation, donated for tax benefits, or used in the wide spectrum of other ways.

Institutions and museums are another group that has become increasingly interested in silver dollars in recent years. As noted earlier, the tax benefits for individuals donating silver dollars to eligible institutions can be considerable. This makes silver dollars attractive to institutions as well, since it offers another vehicle of receiving donations, even when economic conditions tighten cash flow and reduce cash donations.

Once the institution receives the silver dollars, and returns a receipt for tax deduction purposes to the donor, it is then solely responsible for how the silver dollars are used, as long as the use meets legal requirements. Should the institution wish to, at some later date, it may liquidate the donated silver dollars, pay the appropriate taxes, if any, and use the proceeds in any way that meets the requirements of its charter and by-laws (and applicable laws, of course).

In addition to the tax benefits that accrue to the donor, individuals often use silver dollars as a way to "repay" their *alma mater* for the benefits they may have received as students. It also provides a very public way of contributing to the institution involved, which may be personally important to the donor. Through Metro Coin, Ltd., this author has arranged for the transfer through donation of millions of dollars worth of silver dollars to institutions over the years. These coins have often placed on public display, used for educational purposes, or put to some other public-benefiting use by the institution involved. This not only results in public recognition for the donor, but also adds to the versatility of the uses of silver dollar portfolios.

The Future of Silver Dollar Investing

Since the supply is fixed and limited, and the demand for silver dollars is increasing rapidly, the future of silver dollar investing is even brighter than its past proven record of appreciation. While it is impossible to predict *exactly* the return on investment a potential investor can expect, it is reasonable to assume that the same market conditions (supply and demand) that have increased the value of silver dollars over the years will continue to do so in the future.

An interesting point is the limit of existing silver dollars. Since the U.S. Mint no longer makes the Morgan and Peace silver dollars we recommend to investors, it stands to reason that at some point in the future the supply may literally be completely absorbed. Based on current projections, this author believes that this point wll be reached sometime around the year 2000.

Of course, many other factors will affect this "absorption point." These include the current supply of silver dollars in U.S. Treasury and Mint depositories; the number of silver dollars removed from the market by donation to institutions and museums, and the rate at which silver dollars are purchased. The chart on page 180 graphically shows this author's estimate of when silver dollars could actually *cease* to be publicly available, based on current projections of sales and donations.

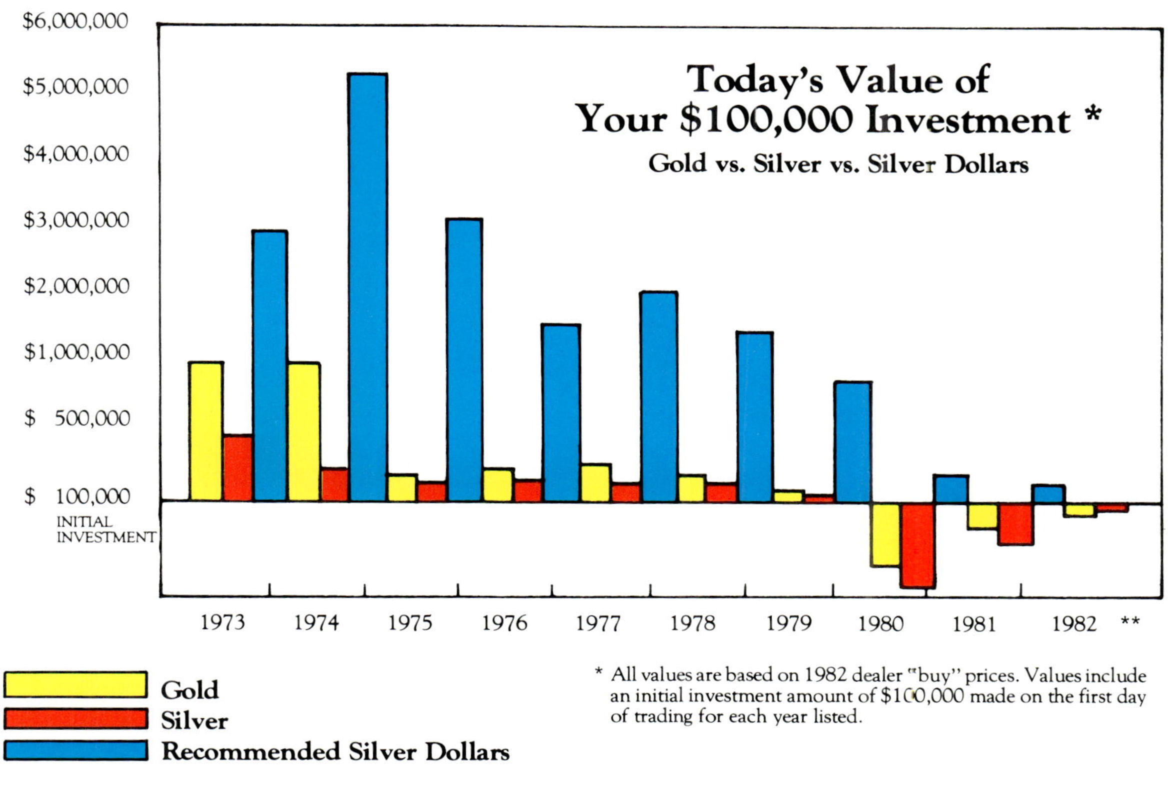

* All values are based on 1982 dealer "buy" prices. Values include an initial investment amount of $100,000 made on the first day of trading for each year listed.

6

A REVIEW OF MORGAN AND PEACE SILVER DOLLARS

Introduction:

There are a number of assumptions underlying this chapter and its extensive review of the individual coins minted in the Morgan and Peace silver dollar series. It is a good idea for the investor to bear these in mind while reading the information, or using this chapter as reference material when considering the purchase of silver dollars for investment purposes. These include:

1) The information contained in this chapter is not based on the cost of the particular coin being discussed, but rather its rarity. As outlined in the grading chapter, the condition of an individual coin determines its grade; while market conditions, such as supply and demand, determine the cost of the coin, based on that grade.

2) The obtainability factor listed for each coin is not based on grade or price, but is based instead on the ease with which it can be located. Some silver dollars are very easy to obtain; while others are so rare that few are ever seen, even by professional numismatists. The easiest to obtain is listed as 1; the most difficult as 10.

3) Investments are a combination of "buyability" and "sellability." No matter what a coin may cost to purchase, it must be resaleable in order to be termed a "complete investment." Many new investors do not take this very vital consideration into account when considering a purchase. However, this factor was involved in the judgements about the investment potential of each coin listed in this chapter.

4) The Approximate Availability listed for each coin is based on an estimate of the *existing* coins in each grade for that year and mint. It is not necessarily a measurement of its obtainability in the current marketplace. This is due to a variety of factors including the number of coins produced, the quantity of each held in private portfolios, and the number that are part of the collections of various institutions around the world. Combined, these factors produce the price of a given coin in a certain condition in the marketplace. Prices for each coin listed in this chapter are appended.

5) This chapter is not intended to sell individual coins. This is an important point for an investor, who may feel that this author has attempted to egrandize any coins that this author may, or may not, have in his own company's inventory. Rather, the intent of this chapter is to outline the characteristics and rarity of each coin in each grade listed. Previous volumes on silver dollar investing have not always taken this view when evaluating individual coins, and a word to the wise should suffice as a caution in that area.

6) The Investment Forecast listed for each coin in each grade is based on the average simple return per year that can be anticipated, based on the three to five year maturity period that this author recommends as a minimum term of investment. This is very important: it is illogical and without foundation to assume that this return is possible in every case within six

months, or in many cases, even one year. With nearly two decades of experience in silver dollar investing, I can state categorically that three to five years is the *minimum term* an investor should consider. Any anticipation of shorter term to maturity can lead to intense frustration for both investor and numismatist, as well as hard feelings. THESE LISTINGS ARE BASED ON EXTREMELY CONSERVATIVE ESTIMATES. PAST HISTORY HAS INDICATED THAT MANY COINS WILL OUTPERFORM THESE FUTURE FORECASTS.

7) A series of charts has been provided in the Appendix section to outline statistical information for each series of silver dollars considered in this book. These charts include the total production of each year and mint; the total mintage by mint mark; the most common coins to obtain; the total number of dies used in each fiscal year's production of silver dollars (a key variable in the number of prooflike dollars produced in a given year); the coins most commonly traded in rolls and as single coins; and the number of proofs produced at the Philadelphia Mint each year during the Morgan series. These charts are designed to provide the same information that is provided on each coin summary page in this chapter in a different format, and should be useful in evaluating each coin relative to its entire series.

8) This chapter includes specific details on the Morgan and Peace series only, and only in the uncirculated grades. This is due to this author's extensive experience with investments in these two series, as well as such considerations as the best coins for investment return purposes and initial investment range. While Seated Liberty, Trade and Early U.S. silver dollars are actively sought and traded by numismatists, they are not considered prime candidates for new investor purchases.

9) It is extremely important to bear in mind that the Morgan and Peace series are entirely different in the eyes of professional numismatists. These two series are graded totally differently (see the grading chapter for more detail); they involved totally different mintages and were produced at different mints in many cases (neither Carson City, nor New Orleans produced *any* Peace silver dollars at all, for example).

Finally, in this chapter fullness of strike and normal surface conditions are listed prominently for each year and mint. Special consideration is given to those factors in terms of an individual year's coins compared with the entire production of that Mint. This means that particular year's coin quality is compared with the entire production of that Mint. For example, an 1885P is an "above average" strike, in terms of fullness, when compared with all other Morgan dollars produced at Philadelphia Mint. As noted above, Morgan and Peace dollars are different in many ways, fullness of strike and normal surface condition production being two of these factors. For this reason, the two series are not compared to each other.

A final important note to remember is which of the mints produced the coins with the most eye appeal. This author's ranking of the best appearing coins in quantity produced by each mint is **Morgan Series:** San Francisco, Philadelphia, Carson City, New Orleans, Denver; **Peace Series:** Philadelphia, Denver, San Francisco.

(All grades listed in this chapter are Mint State unless otherwise noted.)

MORGAN SILVER DOLLARS

SPECIFICATIONS

DESIGNER:	George T. Morgan
WEIGHT:	26.73 grams
COMPOSITION:	.900 silver, .100 copper
DIAMETER:	38.1 mm
MINTS:	Philadelphia, New Orleans, Carson City, Denver, San Francisco
NET WEIGHT:	.77344 oz. pure silver

1878

7 Tail Feather

Statistics

Mintage: 9,759,550 (Includes approximate mintage for 1878 7/8 Tail Feather) (Proof 500)

Fullness of Strike: Average P mint

Normal Surface Conditions: Below average luster, moderate bag marks and abrasions

Approximate Die Varieties: 103 (Includes 8 Tail Feather and 7/8 Tail Feather coins)

Grade:	60	63	64	65	67	69	PL63	PL65
Approximate Availablity	9,500	7,000	6,000	2,500	800	350	1,400	600
Obtainability (Scale of 1 to 10)	3	3	3	4	4	5	3	4

Grade:	60-63	64	65	67-69	PL63	PL65
Investment Forecast: (percentage of return, annual simple interest)	10+	15	25	30	15	25

Investment Desirability by Grade:

MS - 60 MS - 64 MS - 67 MS - 63PL

MS - 63 MS - 65 MS - 69 MS - 65PL

Blue = Superior Red = Excellent Green = Average Black = Below Average

Note: There are two major varieties of this date; one with a concave eagle's breast on the reverse of coins; the other type has the regular convex eagle's breast that appears on coins throughout the remainder of the series.

1878

8 Tail Feather

Statistics

Mintage: 750,000 (Proof 500)

Fullness of Strike: The reverse of 1878 has a concave rather than convex eagle breast feathers

Normal Surface Conditions: Below average luster, moderate bag marks and abrasions

Approximate Die Varieties:

Grade:	**60**	**63**	**64**	**65**	**67**	**69**	**PL63**	**PL65**
Approximate Availablity	10,000	6,000	2,500	2,000	750	300	1,600	650
Obtainability (Scale of 1 to 10)	3	3	4	5	6	7	4	5

Grade:	**60-63**	**64**	**65**	**67-69**	**PL63**	**PL65**
Investment Forecast: (percentage of return, annual simple interest)	10	15	25	25	15	25

Investment Desirability by Grade:

MS - 60 (Black) MS - 64 (Green) MS - 67 (Red) MS - 63PL (Green)

MS - 63 (Green) MS - 65 (Red) MS - 69 (Red) MS - 65PL (Red)

Blue = Superior **Red = Excellent** **Green = Average** **Black = Below Average**

Note: This is the first date and mint striking of the Morgan series. After many coins were produced the eight tail feathers were replaced with seven, the normal odd number of tail feathers. As this change was occurring, the relief of the coin was reduced to a flater design, thus allowing ease of stacking and eliminating many minting problems. Remember, with early day quotas of two million a month production, the first year's dollars will reflect many changes.

1878

7/8 Tail Feather

Statistics

Mintage: 850,000 (estimated)

Fullness of Strike: Average strike for Philadelphia Mint

Normal Surface Conditions: Poor, below average mint luster, moderate bag marks and abrasions

Approximate Die Varieties:

Grade:	60	63	64	65	67	69	PL63	PL65
Approximate Availablity	6,250	5,500	4,500	3,000	1,000	600	1,300	675
Obtainability (Scale of 1 to 10)	3	3	4	4	5	7	3	4

Grade:	60-63	64	65	67-69	PL63	PL65
Investment Forecast: (percentage of return, annual simple interest)	10+	15	30+	30	20	30+

Investment Desirability by Grade:

MS - 60 MS - 64 MS - 67 MS - 63PL

MS - 63 MS - 65 MS - 69 MS - 65PL

Blue = Superior Red = Excellent Green = Average Black = Below Average

Note: The 1878 7/8 Tail Feather was created as the transition from eight tail feathers on the eagle to seven tail feathers. This change in the dies resulted in an overlap of the tail feathers on the eagle. Small changes like this were very common, and when purchasing a 7/8 tail feather make sure that at least four or more tail feathers are showing on the overlapped feathers. Consequently, if less feathers than four are showing, the price should be decreased accordingly.

1878 S

Statistics

Mintage: 9,774,000

Fullness of Strike: Full strike, many choice examples prevail

Normal Surface Conditions: Moderate to heavy bag marks with excellent luster

Approximate Die Varieties: 17

Grade:	60	63	64	65	67	69	PL63	PL65
Approximate Availablity	135,000	240,000	160,000	20,000	4,000	2,000	17,000	9,000
Obtainability (Scale of 1 to 10)	1	2	2	2	2	3	1	2

Grade:	60-63	64	65	67-69	PL63	PL65
Investment Forecast: (percentage of return, annual simple interest)	15	20	25	25	15	25

Investment Desirability by Grade:

MS - 60	MS - 64	MS - 67	MS - 63PL
MS - 63	MS - 65	MS - 69	MS - 65PL

Blue = Superior **Red = Excellent** **Green = Average** **Black = Below Average**

Note: First of a five year run of magnificient looking coins. Although the 1878 is not as nice as the following 1879-82 S Mints, the 1878 is still above average for an S mint dollar. This coin still is in high demand for quantities of choice coins, whether in rolls or singles.

1878 CC

Statistics

Mintage: 2,212,000

Fullness of Strike: Bold full strike majority of the time

Normal Surface Conditions: Average to heavy bag marks and abrasions, average luster

Approximate Die Varieties: 21

Grade:	**60**	**63**	**64**	**65**	**67**	**69**	**PL63**	**PL65**
Approximate Availablity	55,000	16,000	9,000	6,000	2,500	750	11,000	2,000
Obtainability (Scale of 1 to 10)	3	3	3	4	4	6	3	4

Grade:	**60-63**	**64**	**65**	**67-69**	**PL63**	**PL65**
Investment Forecast: (percentage of return, annual simple interest)	15	15+	20+	25	15	25

Investment Desirability by Grade:

[green] MS - 60	[red] MS - 64	[red] MS - 67	[green] MS - 63PL
[green] MS - 63	[red] MS - 65	[red] MS - 69	[red] MS - 65PL

Blue = Superior **Red = Excellent** **Green = Average** **Black = Below Average**

Note: The 1878-CC, the first year of Carson City Mint Morgan Dollars, is struck with the same concave reverse that was mentioned with the 1878 7 Tail Feathers. All the CC dollars of 1878 are struck with very small mint marks, unlike 1879 to '93CC dollars.

1879

Statistics

Mintage: 14,807,100 (Proof 1,100)

Fullness of Strike: Bold full strikes

Normal Surface Conditions: Average bag marks, moderate abrasions, average luster

Approximate Die Varieties: 11

Grade:	60	63	64	65	67	69	PL63	PL65
Approximate Availablity	29,000	17,000	8,000	5,000	2,000	800	9,000	2,100
Obtainability (Scale of 1 to 10)	2	2	3	4	4	4	4	5

Grade:	60-63	64	65	67-69	PL63	PL65
Investment Forecast: (percentage of return, annual simple interest)	10	15	25	30	10-15	25

Investment Desirability by Grade:

MS - 60	MS - 64	MS - 67	MS - 63PL
MS - 63	MS - 65	MS - 69	MS - 65PL

Blue = Superior **Red = Excellent** **Green = Average** **Black = Below Average**

Note: This is the first year of full production of the convex reverses. As will be noted on many of the silver dollars that will follow, the Philadelphia Mint was notorious for using dies long past the capabilities of producing fully struck coins. Thus, while *most* Philadelphia years have large numbers of fully struck available; there are also numerous coins struck from inferior dies.

1879 O

Statistics

Mintage: 2,887,000

Fullness of Strike: Average O mint

Normal Surface Conditions: Heavy bag marks and abrasions

Approximate Die Varieties: 16

Grade:	60	63	64	65	67	69	PL63	PL65
Approximate Availablity	19,000	6,000	4,500	1,000	600	350	2,300	800
Obtainability (Scale of 1 to 10)	3	3	4	6	7	8	6	7

Grade:	60-63	64	65	67-69	PL63	PL65
Investment Forecast: (percentage of return, annual simple interest)	10	15	20	20	10	25

Investment Desirability by Grade:

MS - 60 (Black)	MS - 64 (Green)	MS - 67 (Green)	MS - 63PL (Black)
MS - 63 (Black)	MS - 65 (Green)	MS - 69 (Green)	MS - 65PL (Red)

Blue = Superior **Red = Excellent** **Green = Average** **Black = Below Average**

Note: The first year of production of the New Orleans mint for Morgan dollars. Similarly, the 1879Os in many respects have the same characteristics as the '80O dollars. Both have commanded large premiums over other O mint dollars, but these often leave investors wishing they could find the same quantity and quality as the 1881-'88-O dollars.

1879 S

Statistics

Mintage: 9,110,000

Fullness of Strike: Excellent full strikes

Normal Surface Conditions: Light bag marks and abrasions, excellent above average luster

Approximate Die Varieties: 19

Grade:	**60**	**63**	**64**	**65**	**67**	**69**	**PL63**	**PL65**
Approximate Availablity	105,000	285,000	72,000	27,000	8,000	3,000	70,000	17,000
Obtainability (Scale of 1 to 10)	2	1	1	1	1	1	1	1

Grade:	**60-63**	**64**	**65**	**67-69**	**PL63**	**PL65**
Investment Forecast: (percentage of return, annual simple interest)	15	20	30	30	20	30

Investment Desirability by Grade:

MS - 60 (Green)	MS - 64 (Red)	MS - 67 (Blue)	MS - 63PL (Red)
MS - 63 (Green)	MS - 65 (Blue)	MS - 69 (Blue)	MS - 65PL (Blue)

Blue = Superior **Red = Excellent** **Green = Average** **Black = Below Average**

Note: This begins four more years of superb S mint coins. The 1879-82 are the best strikes and eye appeal of the Morgan series. This, like the other dates (1879-82), may seem to be overlooked because of the ease of acquisition, but their investment future is expectionally bright. Never be afraid of acquiring quantities of this date for investment.

1879 CC

Statistics

Mintage: 756,000

Fullness of Strike: Far below average for CC date. Besides the 80-CC the most unattractive CC date

Normal Surface Conditions: Extremely heavy abrasion and bag marks, wide variation of luster, dull to average

Approximate Die Varieties: 4

Grade:	60	63	64	65	67	69	PL63	PL65
Approximate Availablity	6,500	2,500	1,200	525	205	50	1,125	300
Obtainability (Scale of 1 to 10)	7	8	8	8	8	10	6	8

Grade:	60-63	64	65	67-69	PL63	PL65
Investment Forecast: (percentage of return, annual simple interest)	10	10	25	25	10+	25

Investment Desirability by Grade:

MS - 60 MS - 64 MS - 67 MS - 63PL

MS - 63 MS - 65 MS - 69 MS - 65PL

Blue = Superior **Red = Excellent** **Green = Average** **Black = Below Average**

Note: Two major reverse varieties; the original dies used have very clean and distinct CC mint marks; the second variety has enlarged mint mark letters and by doing this the mint filled old dies and remade large letters in their place, thus causing what is known as the capped "CC" variety, allowing an imprint of both large and small CC letters. This creates an excess metal look, as if this mint work was not genuine. These pieces with the enlarged mint marks (capped variety) definitely do not command the same value as a regular 1879 CC.

1880

Statistics

Mintage: 12,601,355 (Proof 1,355)

Fullness of Strike: Majority of pieces are average to full strikes

Normal Surface Conditions: Average luster, moderate bag marks, moderate to heavy abrasions

Approximate Die Varieties: 24

Grade:	60	63	64	65	67	69	PL63	PL65
Approximate Availablity	52,000	38,000	7,000	4,000	1,800	475	4,200	1,600
Obtainability (Scale of 1 to 10)	2	2	2	3	4	4	4	5

Grade:	60-63	64	65	67-69	PL63	PL65
Investment Forecast: (percentage of return, annual simple interest)	10	15	25	25	15-20	30

Investment Desirability by Grade:

MS - 60 (Black) MS - 64 (Red) MS - 67 (Red) MS - 63PL (Green)

MS - 63 (Green) MS - 65 (Red) MS - 69 (Red) MS - 65PL (Red)

Blue = Superior **Red = Excellent** **Green = Average** **Black = Below Average**

Note: Although this again is a rather high mintage, there are a wide variation of strikes and quality. This is very typical when a large amount of dies were used to produce such a large quantity of a particular year.

1880 O

Statistics

Mintage: 5,305,000

Fullness of Strike: Below average O mint, very flat obverse and reverse

Normal Surface Conditions: Average luster but with extremely heavy bag marks and abrasions

Approximate Die Varieties: 18

Grade:	60	63	64	65	67	69	PL63	PL65
Approximate Availablity	9,000	3,500	2,500	900	200	100	1,900	150
Obtainability (Scale of 1 to 10)	2	3	4	6	8	9	4	6

Grade:	60-63	64	65	67-69	PL63	PL65
Investment Forecast: (percentage of return, annual simple interest)	10	10+	20	30	15+	25

Investment Desirability by Grade:

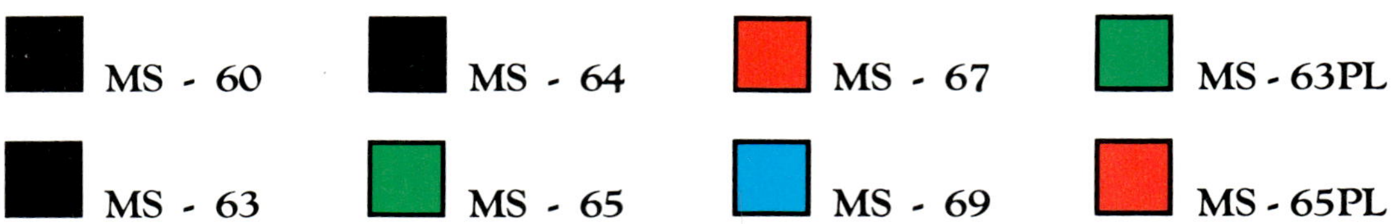

Blue = Superior **Red = Excellent** **Green = Average** **Black = Below Average**

Note: Oddly enough, many of the prooflike coins offered may be "sliders" but have a hard prooflike surface. Unfortunately this is not the case of strong strike throughout the entire series of O mints. As mentioned in 1879O, the 1880O is still not as popular an investment as some would like, because of the difficulty of many people being sold choice AU coins as Mint State pieces. 1879O & 1880O are somewhat problem dates in the public's eye, another reason for consulting a professional.

1880 S

Statistics

Mintage: 8,900,000

Fullness of Strike: As a rule, extremely full strikes

Normal Surface Conditions: Light abrasions and bag marks, magnificent luster

Approximate Die Varieties: 36

Grade:	**60**	**63**	**64**	**65**	**67**	**69**	**PL63**	**PL65**
Approximate Availablity	220,000	465,000	260,000	34,000	7,000	3,500	58,000	17,000
Obtainability (Scale of 1 to 10)	2	1	1	1	1	1	1	1

Grade:	**60-63**	**64**	**65**	**67-69**	**PL63**	**PL65**
Investment Forecast: (percentage of return, annual simple interest)	15	25	30	30	20	30

Investment Desirability by Grade:

Red	MS - 60
Red	MS - 63
Red	MS - 64
Blue	MS - 65
Blue	MS - 67
Blue	MS - 69
Red	MS - 63PL
Blue	MS - 65PL

Blue = Superior **Red = Excellent** **Green = Average** **Black = Below Average**

Note: The second year in a row for *superb quality* from the San Francisco mint. These coins, like the 1879 to '82, are the most generally liked by investors because of the amazing quantities of superb strikes, luster, minimum bag marks, etc., etc., etc. Still an excellent investment because of such on-going popularity.

1880 CC

Statistics

Mintage: 591,000

Fullness of Strike: Poor strike and majority are flat obverse and reverse. Least attractive of the CC dollars

Normal Surface Conditions: Heavy bag marks and abrasions, poor luster

Approximate Die Varieties: 10

Grade:	60	63	64	65	67	69	PL63	PL65
Approximate Availablity	139,000	17,000	9,000	3,000	700	200	2,500	850
Obtainability (Scale of 1 to 10)	2	2	4	5	6	8	4	6

Grade:	60-63	64	65	67-69	PL63	PL65
Investment Forecast: (percentage of return, annual simple interest)	10	20	30	30	15	30

Investment Desirability by Grade:

MS - 60 MS - 64 MS - 67 MS - 63PL

MS - 63 MS - 65 MS - 69 MS - 65PL

Blue = Superior **Red = Excellent** **Green = Average** **Black = Below Average**

Note: There were two major die designs used in striking the '80CC. Again, because of large quotas that were placed on the mint during striking, the overall look of the '80CC has two major differences on the reverse. By using the reverse dies of the '78CC dollar and some filled obverse dies of the '79CC dollar, the '80CC was a composite of varieties to create its total production expectations. This is why it is common to see many different varieties of this year for such a small total mintage.

1881

Statistics

Mintage: 9,163,975 (Proof 975)

Fullness of Strike: Below average for P mint, many flat obverse

Normal Surface Conditions: Light to moderate bag marks and abrasions, luster is above average

Approximate Die Varieties: 11

Grade:	**60**	**63**	**64**	**65**	**67**	**69**	**PL63**	**PL65**
Approximate Availablity	47,000	21,000	11,000	6,700	1,100	650	2,400	1,150
Obtainability (Scale of 1 to 10)	2	2	2	3	3	3	4	5

Grade:	**60-63**	**64**	**65**	**67-69**	**PL63**	**PL65**
Investment Forecast: (percentage of return, annual simple interest)	15	15	25	25	25	30

Investment Desirability by Grade:

MS - 60 MS - 64 MS - 67 MS - 63PL

MS - 63 MS - 65 MS - 69 MS - 65PL

Blue = Superior Red = Excellent Green = Average Black = Below Average

Note: This is a typical P mint dollar, with coins ranging from very flat to full strike, because of the large numbers of coins made on each set of dies. Average P mint dollars in the cases of some of the lesser expensive dollars should be purchased with consideration to strike as well as price. The inexpensive to moderately priced dollar can usually be located in gem quality with a little patience and a positive outlook for future resale value. The common coins in 1970s are many of today's rarities which now command enormous profit.

1881 O

Statistics

Mintage: 5,708,000

Fullness of Strike: Many flat strikes both obverse and reverse
Better than previous two years, but majority still not of full strikes

Normal Surface Conditions: Below average luster, extremely heavy bag marks and abrasions, majority have dull color to coins

Approximate Die Varieties: 11

Grade:	**60**	**63**	**64**	**65**	**67**	**69**	**PL63**	**PL65**
Approximate Availablity	33,000	21,000	8,000	4,100	1,050	500	6,700	1,400
Obtainability (Scale of 1 to 10)	1	1	1	2	3	3	2	2

Grade:	**60-63**	**64**	**65**	**67-69**	**PL63**	**PL65**
Investment Forecast: (percentage of return, annual simple interest)	10+	15+	25	30	15	25

Investment Desirability by Grade:

Green: **MS - 60**	Red: **MS - 64**	Blue: **MS - 67**	Green: **MS - 63PL**
Green: **MS - 63**	Red: **MS - 65**	Blue: **MS - 69**	Red: **MS - 65PL**

Blue = Superior **Red = Excellent** **Green = Average** **Black = Below Average**

Note: Most likely the first New Orleans Morgan dollar to receive large interest. This date is still moderately priced with a large profit potential in gem categories. Many rolls are obtainable at this time although the highest demand is still for gem quality singles.

1881 S

Statistics

Mintage: 12,760,000

Fullness of Strike: The fullest strike of all Morgan dollars

Normal Surface Conditions: Magnificent luster, light-minimum bag marks and abrasions

Approximate Die Varieties: 21

Grade:	60	63	64	65	67	69	PL63	PL65
Approximate Availablity	165,000	485,000	375,000	38,000	9,000	4,500	85,000	22,000
Obtainability (Scale of 1 to 10)	2	1	1	1	1	1	1	1

Grade:	60-63	64	65	67-69	PL63	PL65
Investment Forecast: (percentage of return, annual simple interest)	10-15	20	25	25	20	25

Investment Desirability by Grade:

MS - 60	MS - 64	MS - 67	MS - 63PL
MS - 63	MS - 65	MS - 69	MS - 65PL

Blue = Superior **Red = Excellent** **Green = Average** **Black = Below Average**

Note: With second highest mintage of all S mint Morgans, this date is easy to locate in gem quality. This is the ideal date that all collectors and investors alike would agree is the nicest looking of all mint state Morgan dollars. With incredible striking and luster, just a small handfull of other dates can come close to the overall eye appeal of this date. Do not let this date mislead; in potential, the '81S is a consistent money maker.

1881 CC

Statistics

Mintage: 296,000

Fullness of Strike: Choice CC strike; major are full

Normal Surface Conditions: Full luster and moderate to heavy bag marks and abrasions

Approximate Die Varieties: 3

Grade:	60	63	64	65	67	69	PL63	PL65
Approximate Availablity	127,000	49,000	18,000	6,000	1,850	900	4,500	3,250
Obtainability (Scale of 1 to 10)	2	2	3	4	4	5	3	5

Grade:	60-63	64	65	67-69	PL63	PL65
Investment Forecast: (percentage of return, annual simple interest)	15	15+	20	25	15	25

Investment Desirability by Grade:

MS - 60	MS - 64	MS - 67	MS - 63PL
MS - 63	MS - 65	MS - 69	MS - 65PL

Blue = Superior **Red = Excellent** **Green = Average** **Black = Below Average**

Note: For a CC, as well as all mints, the very low mintage is somewhat deceiving. This as well as the other CC dates, was among the great government CC hoard and over half the total mintage was released through government sales. Although not considered a very common CC date, it would fall into the middle class of obtainability.

Group A, common: 1882, '83, '84; Group B, middle: 1880, '81, '85, '90, '91; Group C, rarest: 1879, '89, '92, '93.

1882

Statistics

Mintage: 11,101,100 (Proof 1,100)

Fullness of Strike: A typical P mint, often reverse flatness

Normal Surface Conditions: Exceptionally heavy bag marks and abrasions, average luster

Approximate Die Varieties: 15

Grade:	**60**	**63**	**64**	**65**	**67**	**69**	**PL63**	**PL65**
Approximate Availablity	45,000	19,000	7,000	4,750	1,300	780	1,950	875
Obtainability (Scale of 1 to 10)	2	2	3	3	3	4	3	4

Grade:	**60-63**	**64**	**65**	**67-69**	**PL63**	**PL65**
Investment Forecast: (percentage of return, annual simple interest)	10-15	15+	20	25	20	30

Investment Desirability by Grade:

MS - 60 **MS - 64** **MS - 67** **MS - 63PL**

MS - 63 **MS - 65** **MS - 69** **MS - 65PL**

Blue = Superior **Red = Excellent** **Green = Average** **Black = Below Average**

Note: Many people might believe that since this is a high mintage, the majority of all the coins would be exceptionally flat since large quantities were struck per die pair. These are easy to locate with flat strikes, but with a little effort a quantity of nice full P mint strike coins can be located. The '82P has close characteristics to other early Philadelphia dollars, i.e. 1879', '80, '81, '83, '84.

1882 O

Statistics

Mintage: 6,090,000

Fullness of Strike: Obverse slightly weak strike, reverse exceptionally flat

Normal Surface Conditions: Below average luster, moderate bag marks and abrasions

Approximate Die Varieties: 21

Grade:	60	63	64	65	67	69	PL63	PL65
Approximate Availablity	66,000	21,000	9,500	6,000	1,700	700	6,500	3,750
Obtainability (Scale of 1 to 10)	2	2	2	3	4	4	2	3

Grade:	60-63	64	65	67-69	PL63	PL65
Investment Forecast: (percentage of return, annual simple interest)	15	20	20	25	25	30

Investment Desirability by Grade:

MS - 60 MS - 64 MS - 67 MS - 63PL

MS - 63 MS - 65 MS - 69 MS - 65PL

Blue = Superior **Red = Excellent** **Green = Average** **Black = Below Average**

Note: This date contains various die varieties, some of which can be seen without magnification. For the true enthusiast on varieties, this date will be very intriguing. A coin that has a properous future, especially in the gem categories.

1882 S

Statistics

Mintage: 9,250,000

Fullness of Strike: Majority found in this date are full strikes

Normal Surface Conditions: Exceptional luster, minimum bag marks and light abrasions

Approximate Die Varieties: 14

Grade:	**60**	**63**	**64**	**65**	**67**	**69**	**PL63**	**PL65**
Approximate Availablity	265,000	305,000	192,000	38,000	6,000	3,500	60,000	20,000
Obtainability (Scale of 1 to 10)	2	1	1	2	2	2	1	2

Grade:	**60-63**	**64**	**65**	**67-69**	**PL63**	**PL65**
Investment Forecast: (percentage of return, annual simple interest)	15	20	30	30	15+	20

Investment Desirability by Grade:

MS - 60 MS - 64 MS - 67 MS - 63PL

MS - 63 MS - 65 MS - 69 MS - 65PL

Blue = Superior **Red = Excellent** **Green = Average** **Black = Below Average**

Note: Last of the common date S mints (1878-82). These last four years are the most easily acquired in quantity of the S mint series, in all grades of mint states. Once again, it is important to keep in mind that because the last five year (1878-82s) are referred to as common does not mean that their investment potential is not far greater than many "rare dates."

1882 CC

Statistics

Mintage: 1,133,000

Fullness of Strike: Majority are well struck, many of the governmental hoard were weakly struck

Normal Surface Conditions: Bag marks are heavy, abrasions moderate, average luster

Approximate Die Varieties: 4

Grade:	60	63	64	65	67	69	PL63	PL65
Approximate Availablity	385,000	218,000	74,000	17,000	6,000	2,000	11,000	4,500
Obtainability (Scale of 1 to 10)	2	2	3	3	4	4	3	4

Grade:	60-63	64	65	67-69	PL63	PL65
Investment Forecast: (percentage of return, annual simple interest)	10+	20	20	25	30	30

Investment Desirability by Grade:

MS - 60 (Green)	MS - 64 (Red)	MS - 67 (Red)	MS - 63PL (Green)
MS - 63 (Red)	MS - 65 (Red)	MS - 69 (Blue)	MS - 65PL (Blue)

Blue = Superior **Red = Excellent** **Green = Average** **Black = Below Average**

Note: The '82CC begins three years that are known as the common Carson City dollar. More than 600,000 were available through the government CC sales. This date, as well as '83 and '84, are often used for promotional campaigns, therefore, they have fluctuated in price in recent years.

1883

Statistics

Mintage: 12,291,039 (Proof 1,039)

Fullness of Strike: Unlike most P mints, '83 is somewhat a soft strike, with many reverse flat strikes

Normal Surface Conditions: Heavy bag marks and abrasions, above average luster, many semi-prooflike conditions

Approximate Die Varieties: 6

Grade:	60	63	64	65	67	69	PL63	PL65
Approximate Availablity	52,000	17,000	13,000	7,000	1,000	400	16,000	4,500
Obtainability (Scale of 1 to 10)	2	2	3	5	5	7	3	5

Grade:	60-63	64	65	67-69	PL63	PL65
Investment Forecast: (percentage of return, annual simple interest)	10	20	25	30	10-15	25

Investment Desirability by Grade:

MS - 60 MS - 64 MS - 67 MS - 63PL

MS - 63 MS - 65 MS - 69 MS - 65PL

Blue = Superior **Red = Excellent** **Green = Average** **Black = Below Average**

Note: First year of the P mints that has a quantity of prooflike coins available. Many one-sided prooflike coins are obtainable in this date. This date may take a little longer to satisfy the gem dollar investor, but the wait is always rewarded in profits potential.

1883 O

Statistics

Mintage: 8,725,000

Fullness of Strike: Majority are flat strikes, some quantity are full strikes (again, same characteristics as 1884 and '85O mints)

Normal Surface Conditions: Average bag marks and abrasions, average luster

Approximate Die Varieties: 16

Grade:	**60**	**63**	**64**	**65**	**67**	**69**	**PL63**	**PL65**
Approximate Availablity	325,000	260,000	57,000	21,000	3,500	1,200	18,000	6,500
Obtainability (Scale of 1 to 10)	1	1	1	1	1	1	1	1

Grade:	**60-63**	**64**	**65**	**67-69**	**PL63**	**PL65**
Investment Forecast: (percentage of return, annual simple interest)	15	15+	30	30	20	30

Investment Desirability by Grade:

MS - 60 MS - 64 MS - 67 MS - 63PL

MS - 63 MS - 65 MS - 69 MS - 65PL

Blue = Superior **Red = Excellent** **Green = Average** **Black = Below Average**

Note: With regard to die varieties, the '82 and '83 New Orleans dollars are very similar. Naturally, the '83O is grouped with the '84O and '85O and both referred to as common dates. Again, the use of the word "common" implies only the obtainability, because the profit potential is great.

1883 S

Statistics

Mintage: 6,250,000

Fullness of Strike: Another S mint strong strike, although many people try to sell AU-55 coins as Mint State pieces and claim it is a weak strike date.

Normal Surface Conditions: An S mint luster, heavy bag marks, average abrasions

Approximate Die Varieties: 2

Grade:	60	63	64	65	67	69	PL63	PL65
Approximate Availablity	4,100	1,750	800	600	150	60	975	310
Obtainability (Scale of 1 to 10)	6	7	7	8	9	10	8	9

Grade:	60-63	64	65	67-69	PL63	PL65
Investment Forecast: (percentage of return, annual simple interest)	10+	15	25	25	15	20+

Investment Desirability by Grade:

MS - 60   MS - 64   MS - 67   MS - 63PL

MS - 63   MS - 65   MS - 69   MS - 65PL

Blue = Superior   **Red = Excellent**   **Green = Average**   **Black = Below Average**

Note: First rare and difficult San Francisco dollar of this series to obtain in Mint State. The true mint state '83S is extremely hard to locate, and a difficult date for many investors to purchase, due to the vast differences in price from an early mintage San Francisco dollar with near equal total mintage. The true differences becomes apparent when the total number of remaining coins are examined.

1883 CC

Statistics

Mintage: 1,204,000

Fullness of Strike: Majority are very nice full strikes

Normal Surface Conditions: Extremely heavy bag marks, heavy abrasions, average luster

Approximate Die Varieties: 4

Grade:	**60**	**63**	**64**	**65**	**67**	**69**	**PL63**	**PL65**
Approximate Availablity	575,000	160,000	70,000	8,000	1,500	550	6,250	3,500
Obtainability (Scale of 1 to 10)	3	3	3	5	5	5	2	3

Grade:	**60-63**	**64**	**65**	**67-69**	**PL63**	**PL65**
Investment Forecast: (percentage of return, annual simple interest)	15+	20	20+	20+	15	20+

Investment Desirability by Grade:

MS - 60 **MS - 64** **MS - 67** **MS - 63PL**

MS - 63 **MS - 65** **MS - 69** **MS - 65PL**

Blue = Superior **Red = Excellent** **Green = Average** **Black = Below Average**

Note: With more than ¾ million (756,000 to be exact) 83-CC dollars in the government hoards, this date, despite the relatively low total mintage, is treated as "common." Like its' '82 and '84 Carson City sister dates, nice specimums are good investments.

1884

Statistics

Mintage: 14,070,875 (Proof 875)

Fullness of Strike: Nice bold P mint strike, very full, nice quality. Many dies used in this year had clashed dies varieties

Normal Surface Conditions: Heavy bag marks, moderate to heavy abrasions, average luster

Approximate Die Varieties: 7

Grade:	**60**	**63**	**64**	**65**	**67**	**69**	**PL63**	**PL65**
Approximate Availablity	22,000	18,000	9,000	4,000	2,000	750	800	400
Obtainability (Scale of 1 to 10)	3	3	3	4	4	5	6	7

Grade:	**60-63**	**64**	**65**	**67-69**	**PL63**	**PL65**
Investment Forecast: (percentage of return, annual simple interest)	15	15	25+	30	20	30

Investment Desirability by Grade:

MS - 60 MS - 64 MS - 67 MS - 63PL

MS - 63 MS - 65 MS - 69 MS - 65PL

Blue = Superior **Red = Excellent** **Green = Average** **Black = Below Average**

Note: Again, even though mintage figures are extremely high for a P mint, this coin is considered slightly better than average Philadelphia dates. The common dates consist of 1896, '97, '98 P, 1886, '87 P, 1888, '89, 1900 P. In respect to common P mints just listed the next groups of P mint dates to locate would consist of 1878, '79, '80, '81, '82, '83, '84, '90, '99, '02, '03. With regards to the last group, the most difficult to find, the most expensive would consist of 1891, '92, '93, '94, '95, '01, '04.

1884 O

Statistics

Mintage: 9,730,000

Fullness of Strike: Average O mint, majority somewhat less than full strikes, although large quantities of full strikes do exist

Normal Surface Conditions: Very similar to '83 and '85 O. Average luster, moderate bag marks, average abrasions

Approximate Die Varieties: 19

Grade:	**60**	**63**	**64**	**65**	**67**	**69**	**PL63**	**PL65**
Approximate Availablity	330,000	242,000	50,000	22,000	6,000	1,400	14,000	3,500
Obtainability (Scale of 1 to 10)	1	1	1	1	1	1	1	1

Grade:	**60-63**	**64**	**65**	**67-69**	**PL63**	**PL65**
Investment Forecast: (percentage of return, annual simple interest)	15	20	30	30	15	25+

Investment Desirability by Grade:

MS - 60	**MS - 64**	**MS - 67**	**MS - 63PL**
MS - 63	**MS - 65**	**MS - 69**	**MS - 65PL**

Blue = Superior **Red = Excellent** **Green = Average** **Black = Below Average**

Note: As mentioned on the 83-O, the 84-O makes up a large amount of the common New Orleans dollars seen today. This date can be acquired in quantity, and should be looked at as a gift because of the rewarding past as well as what the future holds for the 83-84-85-O dollars.

1884 S

Statistics

Mintage: 3,200,000

Fullness of Strike: Not an average S mint, majority are very weak strikes

Normal Surface Conditions: Poor quality luster, moderate bag marks, average abrasions

Approximate Die Varieties: 4

Grade:	**60**	**63**	**64**	**65**	**67**	**69**	**PL63**	**PL65**
Approximate Availablity	475	150	60	15-20	3-4	1-2	6-10	1-2
Obtainability (Scale of 1 to 10)	9	9	10	10	10	10	10	10

Grade:	**60-63**	**64**	**65**	**67-69**	**PL63**	**PL65**
Investment Forecast: (percentage of return, annual simple interest)	10	15	20	35	30	30

Investment Desirability by Grade:

MS - 60 (Black)	MS - 64 (Green)	MS - 67 (Blue)	MS - 63PL (Blue)
MS - 63 (Black)	MS - 65 (Red)	MS - 69 (Blue)	MS - 65PL (Blue)

Blue = Superior **Red = Excellent** **Green = Average** **Black = Below Average**

Note: This coin is extremely difficult to locate in gem quality. The Approximate Availability is very sketchy seeing as how many decades of auction records were examined, as well as nearly two decades of personal observations, and less than a dozen gems and prooflike gem quality coins of the '84-S have been found. A small amount of semi-prooflike coins do exist, but these also are truly difficulty to locate.

1884 CC

Statistics

Mintage: 1,136,000

Fullness of Strike: A CC mint strike, the majority are full strikes

Normal Surface Conditions: Extremely heavy bag marks and abrasions, average luster

Approximate Die Varieties: 9

Grade:	**60**	**63**	**64**	**65**	**67**	**69**	**PL63**	**PL65**
Approximate Availablity	635,000	285,000	98,000	40,000	9,000	3,000	32,000	15,000
Obtainability (Scale of 1 to 10)	1	1	1	2	3	3	2	2

Grade:	**60-63**	**64**	**65**	**67-69**	**PL63**	**PL65**
Investment Forecast: (percentage of return, annual simple interest)	15+	15+	20	25	15+	25

Investment Desirability by Grade:

MS - 60	**MS - 64**	**MS - 67**	**MS - 63PL**
MS - 63	**MS - 65**	**MS - 69**	**MS - 65PL**

Blue = Superior **Red = Excellent** **Green = Average** **Black = Below Average**

Note: Last of the common Carson City dollars. As previously mentioned, total production mintage figures are very deceiving. The 84-CC had an incredible 965,000 coins stored in government vaults that were sold through the Treasury sales. This date has an enviable price per total produced, due to the ratio of availability to demand.

1885

Statistics

Mintage: 17,787,767 (Proof 930)

Fullness of Strike: Very full strike, above average P mint

Normal Surface Conditions: Excellent luster for P mint, moderate bag marks and abrasions. Many of the same characteristics as the 1886-P

Approximate Die Varieties: 10

Grade:	**60**	**63**	**64**	**65**	**67**	**69**	**PL63**	**PL65**
Approximate Availablity	290,000	260,000	58,000	21,500	3,000	1,400	16,000	7,000
Obtainability (Scale of 1 to 10)	1	1	1	1	2	2	1	1

Grade:	**60-63**	**64**	**65**	**67-69**	**PL63**	**PL65**
Investment Forecast: (percentage of return, annual simple interest)	15	15	25-30	30+	20	30+

Investment Desirability by Grade:

- [Red] MS - 60
- [Red] MS - 63
- [Red] MS - 64
- [Blue] MS - 65
- [Blue] MS - 67
- [Blue] MS - 69
- [Red] MS - 63PL
- [Blue] MS - 65PL

Blue = Superior **Red = Excellent** **Green = Average** **Black = Below Average**

Note: This date, as well as the 1885-O, make this year the only year of this decade that can be collected in two different mints in quantity. Many investors should take advantage of this unusual opportunity in all grades MS-60 through MS-65PL. Often small amounts can be purchased, but don't let the ease of obtaining make someone believe this is an inferior investment. Just the opposite is the case.

1885 O

Statistics

Mintage: 9,185,000

Fullness of Strike: Much better than 1883 or 1884 O mints, still occasionally large quantities of flat strikes, although this coin often comes with fully struck coins

Normal Surface Conditions: Moderate bag marks, average abrasions, good to excellent luster

Approximate Die Varieties: 9

Grade:	**60**	**63**	**64**	**65**	**67**	**69**	**PL63**	**PL65**
Approximate Availablity	315,000	265,000	55,000	19,500	2,000	900	18,000	7,500
Obtainability (Scale of 1 to 10)	1	1	2	2	2	4	1	1

Grade:	**60-63**	**64**	**65**	**67-69**	**PL63**	**PL65**
Investment Forecast: (percentage of return, annual simple interest)	15	15	25-30	30+	15-20	30

Investment Desirability by Grade:

MS - 60   MS - 64   MS - 67   MS - 63PL

MS - 63   MS - 65   MS - 69   MS - 65PL

Blue = Superior   **Red = Excellent**   **Green = Average**   **Black = Below Average**

Note: This is the second half of the '85-P and '85-O same year and different mint availability. Only three other times throughout the entire Morgan series is it possible to collect two mints of the same date in quantity at "common" prices. First, 1878 (P & S); second, 1885 (P & O); third, 1898 (P & O); and fourth, 1900 (P & O). Also, it should be noted that investors in this common date have received very promising profits, and gems of this date are always in popular demand.

1885 S

Statistics

Mintage: 1,497,000

Fullness of Strike: Below average S mint characteristics, majority are not completely bold on both obverse and reverse

Normal Surface Conditions: Heavy bag marks and abrasions, nice full luster

Approximate Die Varieties: 6

Grade:	**60**	**63**	**64**	**65**	**67**	**69**	**PL63**	**PL65**
Approximate Availablity	19,000	7,000	2,500	950	250	60	1,175	425
Obtainability (Scale of 1 to 10)	4	4	5	6	6	8	5	6

Grade:	**60-63**	**64**	**65**	**67-69**	**PL63**	**PL65**
Investment Forecast: (percentage of return, annual simple interest)	10	10	20	35	10+	25+

Investment Desirability by Grade:

MS - 60	**MS - 64**	**MS - 67**	**MS - 63PL**
MS - 63	**MS - 65**	**MS - 69**	**MS - 65PL**

Blue = Superior **Red = Excellent** **Green = Average** **Black = Below Average**

Note: Many inferior coins can be found in the marketplace, but a true gem will command a high premium. A hard coin to invest money in and try to resell at a later date, if the coin is not completely a gem.

1885 CC

Statistics

Mintage: 228,000

Fullness of Strike: Typical full struck CC, much like the 1880 through '85 CC

Normal Surface Conditions: Average to heavy bag marks, nice average luster, moderate abrasions.

Approximate Die Varieties: 3

Grade:	**60**	**63**	**64**	**65**	**67**	**69**	**PL63**	**PL65**
Approximate Availablity	145,000	38,000	10,000	3,800	1,300	450	5,500	3,200
Obtainability (Scale of 1 to 10)	3	3	4	5	5	7	4	5

Grade:	**60-63**	**64**	**65**	**67-69**	**PL63**	**PL65**
Investment Forecast: (percentage of return, annual simple interest)	10-15	15+	25	30	15	25-30

Investment Desirability by Grade:

MS - 60 | MS - 64 | MS - 67 | MS - 63PL

MS - 63 | MS - 65 | MS - 69 | MS - 65PL

Blue = Superior **Red = Excellent** **Green = Average** **Black = Below Average**

Note: This coin is similar to the 1881-CC in that there are never large hoards of circulated coins traded. This is unlike the condition for both dates in grades MS-60 through 64. Many novices are drawn to this date due to its overall low mintage. Again, this coin is not hard to acquire in grade of MS-60 to 64. Over 150,000 coins were available through the government hoards, which makes it very similar to the '80-'81 Carson City Dollars.

1886

Statistics

Mintage: 19,963,886 (Proof 886)

Fullness of Strike: This date, as well as the 1885, are the two most prominent, fully struck P mint; the majority far above average

Normal Surface Conditions: Excellent luster, minimum to moderate bag marks, light abrasions

Approximate Die Varieties: 15

Grade:	60	63	64	65	67	69	PL63	PL65
Approximate Availablity	405,000	215,000	40,000	21,000	3,000	1,200	8,500	4,500
Obtainability (Scale of 1 to 10)	1	1	3	4	6	6	3	4

Grade:	60-63	64	65	67-69	PL63	PL65
Investment Forecast: (percentage of return, annual simple interest)	15	20	30	30	15	30

Investment Desirability by Grade:

MS - 60	MS - 64	MS - 67	MS - 63PL
MS - 63	MS - 65	MS - 69	MS - 65PL

Blue = Superior **Red = Excellent** **Green = Average** **Black = Below Average**

Note: As in most P mints, near the end of a die's lifetime there are many flat coins produced. The 1886-P is no exception. The problem is that many nice coins do exist in full strike, as well as flatter strike MS-63 and -64 coins. Many people often confuse the issue and think that the majority of 1886-P are flat. This is totally untrue.

1886 O

Statistics

Mintage: 10,710,000

Fullness of Strike: The typical strike is average to above average. Many people disagree, but there are quantities of fully struck AU specimens to justify the nice original full strikes

Normal Surface Conditions: Heavy bag marks, below average luster with moderate to heavy abrasions

Approximate Die Varieties: 10

Grade:	**60**	**63**	**64**	**65**	**67**	**69**	**PL63**	**PL65**
Approximate Availablity	9,500	1,000	600	300	20	3 to 5	125	10
Obtainability (Scale of 1 to 10)	6	8	8	10	10	10	9	10

Grade:	**60-63**	**64**	**65**	**67-69**	**PL63**	**PL65**
Investment Forecast: (percentage of return, annual simple interest)	10	10	30+	35+	15+	30+

Investment Desirability by Grade:

MS - 60	MS - 64	MS - 67	MS - 63PL
MS - 63	MS - 65	MS - 69	MS - 65PL

Blue = Superior **Red = Excellent** **Green = Average** **Black = Below Average**

Note: This date also has many of the same characteristics that some of the other more expensive New Orleans Dollars exhibit (i.e. 1892-O, 1893-O, 1894-O, 1895-O, 1897-O). Again, this is a coin suggested to be acquired in gem BU condition because of its unpopularity with many dealers and collectors who have searched for many years and settled for an inferior, lower grade coin. If a 1886-O is in your future, don't hesitate to set new records obtaining that right coin.

1886 S

Statistics

Mintage: 750,000

Fullness of Strike: Below average for S mint, although some quantities have turned up with the average bold S mint characteristics

Normal Surface Conditions: Moderate bag marks, minimum abrasions, average luster

Approximate Die Varieties: 3

Grade:	60	63	64	65	67	69	PL63	PL65
Approximate Availablity	19,000	3,500	3,000	900	450	50	1,850	525
Obtainability (Scale of 1 to 10)	5	5	6	7	8	9	6	7

Grade:	60-63	64	65	67-69	PL63	PL65
Investment Forecast: (percentage of return, annual simple interest)	10	10	15-20	30	10	25-30

Investment Desirability by Grade:

MS - 60	MS - 64	MS - 67	MS - 63PL
MS - 63	MS - 65	MS - 69	MS - 65PL

Blue = Superior **Red = Excellent** **Green = Average** **Black = Below Average**

Note: Oddly enough, this coin does not produce high returns in lower grades than Mint State 65. This coin is therefore overlooked many times by an investor because it infrequently appears in the marketplace in Mint State 65 or better. Because of its relative low total mintage, popularity is gained only through gem Mint State 65 or better coins.

1887

Statistics

Mintage: 20,290,710 (Proof 710)

Fullness of Strike: Average P mint, not nearly as fully struck as its predecessor, the 1885 and '86-P

Normal Surface Conditions: Moderate bag marks, minimum abrasions, average luster

Approximate Die Varieties: 14

Grade:	**60**	**63**	**64**	**65**	**67**	**69**	**PL63**	**PL65**
Approximate Availablity	390,000	260,000	40,000	19,000	3,000	1,000	8,000	4,200
Obtainability (Scale of 1 to 10)	1	2	3	3	3	4	2	3

Grade:	**60-63**	**64**	**65**	**67-69**	**PL63**	**PL65**
Investment Forecast: (percentage of return, annual simple interest)	15	20+	30	35	15-20	30

Investment Desirability by Grade:

MS - 60 **MS - 64** **MS - 67** **MS - 63PL**

MS - 63 **MS - 65** **MS - 69** **MS - 65PL**

Blue = Superior **Red = Excellent** **Green = Average** **Black = Below Average**

Note: Along with the '85 and '86, the '87 is usually an investor's first purchase in the P mint series. Somewhat easy to locate with an excellent track record of popularity and profit, the '85-'87 Philadelphia mints bring much attention among silver dollar investors.

1887 O

Statistics

Mintage: 11,550,000

Fullness of Strike: Very flat strikes, some pieces have minimum bag marks with absolutely terrible strikes

Normal Surface Conditions: Excessively heavy bag marks, below average luster, not an overall attractive coin the majority of time

Approximate Die Varieties: 10

Grade:	60	63	64	65	67	69	PL63	PL65
Approximate Availablity	50,000	6,000	3,000	1,800	100	35	3,500	1,100
Obtainability (Scale of 1 to 10)	3	3	6	7	7	9	6	7

Grade:	60-63	64	65	67-69	PL63	PL65
Investment Forecast: (percentage of return, annual simple interest)	10	15	25+	30+	10-15	30+

Investment Desirability by Grade:

MS - 60	MS - 64	MS - 67	MS - 63PL
MS - 63	MS - 65	MS - 69	MS - 65PL

Blue = Superior **Red = Excellent** **Green = Average** **Black = Below Average**

Note: This coin is highly recommended in gem category, but is not advised in lower uncirculated grades. The popularity of this coin is extremely low for average mint state coins. A person might tend to believe that with a high amount minted there would be an over abundance of gems waiting for the investor — this is *definitely* not the case.

1887 S

Statistics

Mintage: 1,771,000

Fullness of Strike: Above average S mint, often reverse not as bold as obverse

Normal Surface Conditions: Moderate bag marks, often excessive abrasions, average luster

Approximate Die Varieties: 5

Grade:	**60**	**63**	**64**	**65**	**67**	**69**	**PL63**	**PL65**
Approximate Availablity	16,000	9,000	6,000	2,750	650	175	2,750	875
Obtainability (Scale of 1 to 10)	3	3	5	7	7	8	4	6

Grade:	**60-63**	**64**	**65**	**67-69**	**PL63**	**PL65**
Investment Forecast: (percentage of return, annual simple interest)	10	10	20	30	10	25+

Investment Desirability by Grade:

MS - 60	Black
MS - 63	Black
MS - 64	Black
MS - 65	Red
MS - 67	Red
MS - 69	Blue
MS - 63PL	Black
MS - 65PL	Red

Blue = Superior **Red = Excellent** **Green = Average** **Black = Below Average**

Note: The 1887-S, as well as the 1888-S are notorious for over-polished dies. This caused striations, and many are one-sided prooflike coins. Gem pieces of 1887-S and 1888-S do exist, and are worth seeking out as an investment if you enjoy the true challenge of locating these two elusive dates.

1888

Statistics

Mintage: 19,183,333 (Proof 832)

Fullness of Strike: Another year that carries two major varieties: 1) Very poor struck, horribly flat and very little detail; 2) the average P mint with nice quality that is customarily like 1885 to '87 coin

Normal Surface Conditions: Majority are moderate to heavy bag marks and abrasions, far below average luster

Approximate Die Varieties: 3

Grade:	**60**	**63**	**64**	**65**	**67**	**69**	**PL63**	**PL65**
Approximate Availablity	102,000	47,000	13,100	8,500	1,900	650	3,250	1,850
Obtainability (Scale of 1 to 10)	2	3	3	4	5	5	3	4

Grade:	**60-63**	**64**	**65**	**67-69**	**PL63**	**PL65**
Investment Forecast: (percentage of return, annual simple interest)	10-15	10-15	30	30	15	30

Investment Desirability by Grade:

- Green: **MS - 60**
- Green: **MS - 64**
- Blue: **MS - 67**
- Green: **MS - 63PL**
- Green: **MS - 63**
- Blue: **MS - 65**
- Blue: **MS - 69**
- Blue: **MS - 65PL**

Blue = Superior **Red = Excellent** **Green = Average** **Black = Below Average**

Note: As is characteristic of most Philadelphia dates, this year involved large production and the overuse of dies that should have been replaced long before they actually were. This coin doesn't have large popularity in Mint State grades of 60-64, but MS-65 and better are very sought-after in this date.

1888 O

Statistics

Mintage: 12,150,000

Fullness of Strike: Weak, often exceptionally flat, second year of below average O mints that will continue with full strikes being elusive from 1887 to '97 in New Orleans dates

Normal Surface Conditions: Heavy bag marks, below average luster, moderate to heavy abrasions.

Approximate Die Varieties: 9

Grade:	60	63	64	65	67	69	PL63	PL65
Approximate Availablity	78,000	25,000	8,500	4,000	720	250	3,400	1,250
Obtainability (Scale of 1 to 10)	2	3	3	5	5	5	3	5

Grade:	60-63	64	65	67-69	PL63	PL65
Investment Forecast: (percentage of return, annual simple interest)	10	15	25+	30	10-15	25-30

Investment Desirability by Grade:

MS - 60　MS - 64　MS - 67　MS - 63PL

MS - 63　MS - 65　MS - 69　MS - 65PL

Blue = Superior　**Red = Excellent**　**Green = Average**　**Black = Below Average**

Note: A somewhat common date; many investors "give up" looking for a gem. Searching for gems or prooflike can be a long, but rewarding task. Larger amounts of gems seemed to circulate in the 1970s but are much more difficult to locate in 1980s.

1888 S

Statistics

Mintage: 657,000

Fullness of Strike: Below average S mint, many striations, many flat strikes

Normal Surface Conditions: Heavy bag marks, moderate to heavy abrasions, average luster

Approximate Die Varieties: 3

Grade:	60	63	64	65	67	69	PL63	PL65
Approximate Availablity	9,250	6,750	2,400	1,650	320	100	1,300	475
Obtainability (Scale of 1 to 10)	5	5	6	6	6	8	5	6

Grade:	60-63	64	65	67-69	PL63	PL65
Investment Forecast: (percentage of return, annual simple interest)	10-15	10-15	20	25+	15	20+

Investment Desirability by Grade:

MS - 60	MS - 64	MS - 67	MS - 63PL
MS - 63	MS - 65	MS - 69	MS - 65PL

Blue = Superior **Red = Excellent** **Green = Average** **Black = Below Average**

Note: The 1888-S is commonly located with many striations due to excessively heavy polishing of the dies. Most prooflike coins will have these characteristics, and a true gem 1888-S without obverse or reverse striations is uncommon. Large premiums are always being offered for MS-65 or better coins, and very few ever change hands.

1889

Statistics

Mintage: 21,726,811 (Proof 811)

Fullness of Strike: Below average for P. This may be caused by a large number of coins produced per die pair

Normal Surface Conditions: Average luster, moderate bag marks, minimum abrasions

Approximate Die Varieties: 12

Grade:	60	63	64	65	67	69	PL63	PL65
Approximate Availablity	106,000	63,000	23,000	6,250	1,200	475	6,500	1,500
Obtainability (Scale of 1 to 10)	2	3	3	4	4	5	4	6

Grade:	60-63	64	65	67-69	PL63	PL65
Investment Forecast: (percentage of return, annual simple interest)	15	15	25	30	10-15	30

Investment Desirability by Grade:

MS - 60 MS - 64 MS - 67 MS - 63PL

MS - 63 MS - 65 MS - 69 MS - 65PL

Blue = Superior Red = Excellent Green = Average Black = Below Average

Note: Another example of many coins being produced, but for the amount made vs. amount of gems available, the ratio is very large. A somewhat elusive date, since it is very common to have weak spots on reverse breast feathers and the hair above ear on the obverse in many cases.

1889 O

Statistics

Mintage: 11,875,000

Fullness of Strike: Another average or typical O mint, majority very flat

Normal Surface Conditions: Heavy bag marks and abrasions, average luster

Approximate Die Varieties: 13

Grade:	60	63	64	65	67	69	PL63	PL65
Approximate Availablity	39,000	25,000	3,500	800	60	10-15	475	200
Obtainability (Scale of 1 to 10)	4	6	7	8	9	9	7	9

Grade:	60-63	64	65	67-69	PL63	PL65
Investment Forecast: (percentage of return, annual simple interest)	10	15	25	35	20+	35

Investment Desirability by Grade:

MS - 60 MS - 64 MS - 67 MS - 63PL

MS - 63 MS - 65 MS - 69 MS - 65PL

Blue = Superior **Red = Excellent** **Green = Average** **Black = Below Average**

Note: This coin is similar to the characteristics of the 1891-O. Many very flat strikes, and collectors and investors can search for years to obtain a true gem, and even longer for a prooflike gem. Not an overwhelmingly popular coin, unless it is a gem. When either a prooflike gem '89-O or '91-O reaches auctions, it is always sure to cause widespread interest.

1889 S

Statistics

Mintage: 700,000

Fullness of Strike: Average S mint, majority full strike

Normal Surface Conditions: Minimum to average bag marks, many abrasions, average luster

Approximate Die Varieties: 6

Grade:	60	63	64	65	67	69	PL63	PL65
Approximate Availablity	9,500	4,200	2,800	980	420	165	2,600	820
Obtainability (Scale of 1 to 10)	4	4	5	6	6	7	4	5

Grade:	60-63	64	65	67-69	PL63	PL65
Investment Forecast: (percentage of return, annual simple interest)	10	10	10-15	10-15	10	10-15

Investment Desirability by Grade:

■ (Black) MS - 60	■ (Green) MS - 64	■ (Green) MS - 67	■ (Black) MS - 63PL
■ (Black) MS - 63	■ (Green) MS - 65	■ (Green) MS - 69	■ (Green) MS - 65PL

Blue = Superior **Red = Excellent** **Green = Average** **Black = Below Average**

Note: This coin, because of its overall low mintage, is very deceiving. It is easily found in small hoards, and usually found are fully struck pieces with average luster and bag marks. Full strike minimum bag mark pieces can be elusive, and the search may try the patience of many. This coin has had little publicity and since very few gems ever trade hands, this date doesn't have widespread popularity. There were considerable quantities of this date in the Redfield hoard, but bag marks and abrasions were plentiful.

1889 CC

Statistics

Mintage: 350,000

Fullness of Strike: Average CC date with possibly a small amount of weakly struck coins existing

Normal Surface Conditions: Average bag marks, luster, minimum abrasions

Approximate Die Varieties: 2

Grade:	60	63	64	65	67	69	PL63	PL65
Approximate Availablity	1,350	875	260	55	25	10	175	95
Obtainability (Scale of 1 to 10)	7	7	8	8	8	8	6	7

Grade:	60-63	64	65	67-69	PL63	PL65
Investment Forecast: (percentage of return, annual simple interest)	15	15	15-20	30	10-15	25

Investment Desirability by Grade:

MS - 60 (Green)	MS - 64 (Green)	MS - 67 (Red)	MS - 63PL (Green)
MS - 63 (Green)	MS - 65 (Green)	MS - 69 (Red)	MS - 65PL (Red)

Blue = Superior **Red = Excellent** **Green = Average** **Black = Below Average**

Note: Probably of the more expensive category, this is the most sought after coin by collectors. Many altered dates do exist of this date, and extreme caution should be used when buying this date from anyone other than a professional numismatist. This is the rarest and most expensive of all the CC dollars in the Morgan series.

1890

Statistics

Mintage: 16,802,590 (Proof 590)

Fullness of Strike: Below average P mint, majority are typically weak obverse and reverse

Normal Surface Conditions: Heavy bag marks, moderate abrasions, below average luster

Approximate Die Varieties: 9

Grade:	60	63	64	65	67	69	PL63	PL65
Approximate Availablity	55,000	37,000	16,000	4,000	1,400	850	775	200
Obtainability (Scale of 1 to 10)	3	3	4	5	5	7	5	7

Grade:	60-63	64	65	67-69	PL63	PL65
Investment Forecast: (percentage of return, annual simple interest)	1020	25	35	15	30	30

Investment Desirability by Grade:

MS - 60 MS - 64 MS - 67 MS - 63PL

MS - 63 MS - 65 MS - 69 MS - 65PL

Blue = Superior **Red = Excellent** **Green = Average** **Black = Below Average**

Note: The 1890 to 1894 P mints have many of the same characteristics. Often gems of these dates are exceptionally elusive not to mention prooflike specimens, which are even more difficult to locate. For years, this date was represented as very common, although no large bag quantities have surfaced recently, and the amount of gems is very low.

1890 O

Statistics

Mintage: 10,701,000

Fullness of Strike: Poor, weak strikes, often flat strikes with minimal bag marks

Normal Surface Conditions: Average to heavy bag marks, below average luster, moderate abrasions

Approximate Die Varieties: 9

Grade:	60	63	64	65	67	69	PL63	PL65
Approximate Availablity	24,000	13,000	2,500	1,100	375	75	2,100	600
Obtainability (Scale of 1 to 10)	4	5	6	7	8	9	6	6

Grade:	60-63	64	65	67-69	PL63	PL65
Investment Forecast: (percentage of return, annual simple interest)	10	15	25	30	10	25

Investment Desirability by Grade:

MS - 60 MS - 64 MS - 67 MS - 63PL

MS - 63 MS - 65 MS - 69 MS - 65PL

Blue = Superior **Red = Excellent** **Green = Average** **Black = Below Average**

Note: Many coins of this date are like the usual 1889 to '97-O mints with exceptionally flat strikes, average to heavy bag marks and abrasions. There are few very nice coins of this date, but these are far outnumbered by inferior strikes and luster. Many times investors are offered rolls of minimum bag marks, full luster, very flat strikes. These do not represent as good an investment as the harder to locate gem coins.

1890 S

Statistics

Mintage: 8,230,373

Fullness of Strike: Full S mint characteristics, majority exceptionally nice full strikes

Normal Surface Conditions: Above average luster, light to minimum bag marks and abrasions

Approximate Die Varieties: 12

Grade:	**60**	**63**	**64**	**65**	**67**	**69**	**PL63**	**PL65**
Approximate Availablity	40,000	24,000	18,000	6,500	3,500	850	11,000	3,700
Obtainability (Scale of 1 to 10)	3	3	4	5	5	5	4	5

Grade:	**60-63**	**64**	**65**	**67-69**	**PL63**	**PL65**
Investment Forecast: (percentage of return, annual simple interest)	10	10	20+	30	10-15	15-20

Investment Desirability by Grade:

MS - 60 **MS - 64** **MS - 67** **MS - 63PL**

MS - 63 **MS - 65** **MS - 69** **MS - 65PL**

Blue = Superior **Red = Excellent** **Green = Average** **Black = Below Average**

Note: The '90-S and the '91-S are probably the more popular San Francisco dates to accumulate from the 1890's. These two dates represent the least expensive of that era, and generally can be located with little effort compared to the other S mints in this decade.

1890 CC

Statistics

Mintage: 2,309,041

Fullness of Strike: Nice strike, majority full, similar to the CC, including '82 - '84, '90 - '91

Normal Surface Conditions: Heavy abrasions and bag marks, average luster

Approximate Die Varieties: 8

Grade:	60	63	64	65	67	69	PL63	PL65
Approximate Availablity	13,100	12,600	11,700	2,100	675	275	1,600	600
Obtainability (Scale of 1 to 10)	4	4	5	6	6	7	5	6

Grade:	60-63	64	65	67-69	PL63	PL65
Investment Forecast: (percentage of return, annual simple interest)	15	20	25	25	15-20	20-25

Investment Desirability by Grade:

MS - 60 (Green)	MS - 64 (Red)	MS - 67 (Red)	MS - 63PL (Green)
MS - 63 (Green)	MS - 65 (Red)	MS - 69 (Red)	MS - 65PL (Red)

Blue = Superior **Red = Excellent** **Green = Average** **Black = Below Average**

Note: With respect to the total mintage, a person would tend to believe the Treasury hoard should contain large quantities; oddly enough there were under 4,000 coins in the Treasury Vaults. It is very common to see quantities of circulate '91-CC, but the true gems are scarce.

1891

Statistics

Mintage: 8.694,206 (Proof 650)

Fullness of Strike: Not an average P mint, many weak strikes, below average

Normal Surface Conditions: Moderate to heavy bag marks, heavy abrasions, majority are poor luster and far less attractive than any other P mint date

Approximate Die Varieties: 3

Grade:	60	63	64	65	67	69	PL63	PL65
Approximate Availablity	18,000	3,000	2,000	1,250	485	125	450	65
Obtainability (Scale of 1 to 10)	4	4	4	7	8	9	7	9

Grade:	60-63	64	65	67-69	PL63	PL65
Investment Forecast: (percentage of return, annual simple interest)	10	15+	25+	30+	25	30

Investment Desirability by Grade:

MS - 60 (Black)	MS - 64 (Red)	MS - 67 (Red)	MS - 63PL (Red)
MS - 63 (Black)	MS - 65 (Red)	MS - 69 (Red)	MS - 65PL (Red)

Blue = Superior **Red = Excellent** **Green = Average** **Black = Below Average**

Note: If the search for a gem 91-P is on your horizon, good luck. Coins of this date are often promoted as a higher grade than they really are. This is either done by the lack of true gems on the market to compare to, or the investor gives up his or her long search for a very high yield potential 1891 P gem.

1891 O

Statistics

Mintage: 7,954,529

Fullness of Strike: Exceptionally weak, very poor, flat strike on obverse and reverse

Normal Surface Conditions: Moderate to heavy bag marks, heavy abrasions, average luster

Approximate Die Varieties: 8

Grade:	60	63	64	65	67	69	PL63	PL65
Approximate Availablity	6,900	2,650	435	310	6-8	2-3	160	25
Obtainability (Scale of 1 to 10)	5	7	8	9	10	10	9	10

Grade:	60-63	64	65	67-69	PL63	PL65
Investment Forecast: (percentage of return, annual simple interest)	10-15	15+	25	35	30	35

Investment Desirability by Grade:

MS - 60 MS - 64 MS - 67 MS - 63PL

MS - 63 MS - 65 MS - 69 MS - 65PL

Blue = Superior **Red = Excellent** **Green = Average** **Black = Below Average**

Note: Often small amounts of '91-O are discovered and represented as minimum bag mark gems. Usually these are nice MS-64 coins with less than full strikes. A '91-O can take an investor on a long path before a gem, or especially a prooflike gem, can ever be seen, much less ever purchased. It is amazing the high profits that some have realized over the years by holding onto their elusive profit makers. If you are ever lucky enough to have a gem offered, "step out" and pay a healthy premium.

1891 S

Statistics

Mintage: 5,296,000

Fullness of Strike: Average S mint, nice full strike characteristics

Normal Surface Conditions: Average to heavy bag marks and abrasions, full luster

Approximate Die Varieties: 5

Grade:	60	63	64	65	67	69	PL63	PL65
Approximate Availablity	66,500	31,000	6,500	2,875	750	300	4,500	2,000
Obtainability (Scale of 1 to 10)	3	3	4	6	7	7	5	5

Grade:	60-63	64	65	67-69	PL63	PL65
Investment Forecast: (percentage of return, annual simple interest)	10	10-15	20	30	15	25

Investment Desirability by Grade:

MS - 60	MS - 64	MS - 67	MS - 63PL
MS - 63	MS - 65	MS - 69	MS - 65PL

Blue = Superior **Red = Excellent** **Green = Average** **Black = Below Average**

Note: As mentioned before, very comparable to the 1890-S. These two dates represent the only inexpensive way to own a San Francisco Mint State 65 specimen from the 1890s. Possibly an overlooked coin in MS-65 for many years. A coin to watch in the years to come.

1891 CC

Statistics

Mintage: 1,618,000

Fullness of Strike: Very full strikes, majority of this date are excellent fully struck coins

Normal Surface Conditions: Above average luster, heavy bag marks and abrasions

Approximate Die Varieties: 4

Grade:	60	63	64	65	67	69	PL63	PL65
Approximate Availablity	7,250	5,800	4,500	880	325	200	1,350	425
Obtainability (Scale of 1 to 10)	4	4	4	6	8	8	6	7

Grade:	60-63	64	65	67-69	PL63	PL65
Investment Forecast: (percentage of return, annual simple interest)	10-15	15-20	25	30+	20	30

Investment Desirability by Grade:

MS - 60 MS - 64 MS - 67 MS - 63PL

MS - 63 MS - 65 MS - 69 MS - 65PL

Blue = Superior Red = Excellent Green = Average Black = Below Average

Note: The '91-CC is like the '90-CC with respect to high total mintage, and few coins in the Treasury hoards. Slightly more than 5,000 coins were presented by the government. With this small amount held by the Treasury, it is easy to see why the '91-CC is the most common of circulated Carson City dates.

1892

Statistics

Mintage: 1,037,245 (Proof 1,245)

Fullness of Strike: Again, like various other years, two major types of strikes: 1) One variety are full nice coins; 2) the other variety is below average, very weak

Normal Surface Conditions: Type 1) Light to moderate bag marks, minimum abrasions, average luster; Type 2) luster is usually below normal "P" mint, expect abrasions with light to moderate bag marks

Approximate Die Varieties: 2

Grade:	60	63	64	65	67	69	PL63	PL65
Approximate Availablity	3,400	2,700	1,845	770	210	25	460	175
Obtainability (Scale of 1 to 10)	6	6	6	6	7	8	6	7

Grade:	60-63	64	65	67-69	PL63	PL65
Investment Forecast: (percentage of return, annual simple interest)	15	15+	25	25+	20-25	30+

Investment Desirability by Grade:

MS - 60 MS - 64 MS - 67 MS - 63PL

MS - 63 MS - 65 MS - 69 MS - 65PL

Blue = Superior Red = Excellent Green = Average Black = Below Average

Note: Even though the '92-P doesn't have an extremely high mintage, it is important to point out that dies were used far beyond their capability to produce gem coins. In recent years, this date has received little attention from either promoters and investors. This coin may have reached a price peak, and may have to wait for the next cycle to gain momentum again.

1892 O

Statistics

Mintage: 2,744,000

Fullness of Strike: Below average for O mint, very poor, soft strikes obverse and reverse

Normal Surface Conditions: Heavy bag marks and abrasions, many poor strike MS-60s, with luster below normal

Approximate Die Varieties: 5

Grade:	60	63	64	65	67	69	PL63	PL65
Approximate Availablity	1,850	625	75	30	3-4	1-2	6-7	2-3
Obtainability (Scale of 1 to 10)	5	7	8	9	10	10	9	10

Grade:	60-63	64	65	67-69	PL63	PL65
Investment Forecast: (percentage of return, annual simple interest)	10	10-15	25	25	25	35

Investment Desirability by Grade:

MS - 60	MS - 64	MS - 67	MS - 63PL
MS - 63	MS - 65	MS - 69	MS - 65PL

Blue = Superior **Red = Excellent** **Green = Average** **Black = Below Average**

Note: The fourth year in a row in which large quantities were totally produced. The majority are flat strikes and in undesirable quality compared to their potential in gem quality. These are so elusive that it is hard to comprehend. Many years go by and not one major auction has a full set of New Orleans dollars in Mint State 65.

1892 S

Statistics

Mintage: 1,200,000

Fullness of Strike: Below average of a S mint dollar

Normal Surface Conditions: Average bag marks, minimum to average abrasions, below average luster for S mint

Approximate Die Varieties: 3

Grade:	60	63	64	65	67	69	PL63	PL65
Approximate Availablity	435	220	70	27	6-8	1-2	17-18	8-9
Obtainability (Scale of 1 to 10)	8	8	9	9	10	10	8	9

Grade:	60-63	64	65	67-69	PL63	PL65
Investment Forecast: (percentage of return, annual simple interest)	10	10	15-20	20+	10+	20

Investment Desirability by Grade:

MS - 60	MS - 64	MS - 67	MS - 63PL
MS - 63	MS - 65	MS - 69	MS - 65PL

Blue = Superior **Red = Excellent** **Green = Average** **Black = Below Average**

Note: Very similar to the 1893-S. A mint state example should be authenticated by a very reputable professional numismatist because many alterations of this date are present on the marketplace. With an enormous mintage compared to estimated availability, the '92-S and '93-S always gain popularity at auctions, but seldom do many pieces ever enter the marketplace. Many collectors consider the '92-S as rare as the '93-S, and believe that they both should trade for the same price in Mint State.

1892 CC

Statistics

Mintage: 1,352,000

Fullness of Strike: Average weak strikes, although full strikes are obtainable

Normal Surface Conditions: Moderate bag marks, average luster, light abrasions

Approximate Die Varieties: 7

Grade:	**60**	**63**	**64**	**65**	**67**	**69**	**PL63**	**PL65**
Approximate Availablity	6,700	2,925	1,820	1,300	190	41	375	50
Obtainability (Scale of 1 to 10)	4	5	6	6	8	9	7	9

Grade:	**60-63**	**64**	**65**	**67-69**	**PL63**	**PL65**
Investment Forecast: (percentage of return, annual simple interest)	10	10-15	20	25	15-20	30

Investment Desirability by Grade:

MS - 60 **MS - 64** **MS - 67** **MS - 63PL**

MS - 63 **MS - 65** **MS - 69** **MS - 65PL**

Blue = Superior **Red = Excellent** **Green = Average** **Black = Below Average**

Note: Next to last year of mintage, this date was suspected to be in the Carson City Treasury hoard. Surprisingly there were no '92-CCs in the hoard, and the '92-CC received a tremendous upswing bidding for several years that followed. The '92-CC possibly out-produced itself, and many people are sitting back to watch its performance in the upcoming years. A very difficult coin to locate in Mint State 65 or higher, but always an easy coin to sell.

1893

Statistics

Mintage: 389,792 (Proof 792)

Fullness of Strike: Quite a gamut of strikes from very full to exceptionally flat. Very uneven date due to this range of strikes.

Normal Surface Conditions: Moderate abrasions and bag marks, average luster

Approximate Die Varieties: 5

Grade:	60	63	64	65	67	69	PL63	PL65
Approximate Availablity	3,175	955	820	575	55	12	90	10
Obtainability (Scale of 1 to 10)	7	7	7	8	9	10	8	10

Grade:	60-63	64	65	67-69	PL63	PL65
Investment Forecast: (percentage of return, annual simple interest)	10	10+	15-20	20	20	25

Investment Desirability by Grade:

MS - 60	MS - 64	MS - 67	MS - 63PL
MS - 63	MS - 65	MS - 69	MS - 65PL

Blue = Superior **Red = Excellent** **Green = Average** **Black = Below Average**

Note: Truly a scarce coin in Mint State 65 or better. This date is the third most difficult of all Philadelphia Morgan dollars. It falls behind the 1901-P and the 1894-P. Both of these coins are exceptionally elusive, and very seldom are seen at coin conventions or auctions. This may account for the less activity among today's investor versus the collectors of a decade ago.

1893 O

Statistics

Mintage: 300,000

Fullness of Strike: Average O mint if total mintage is kept in mind, many flat strikes

Normal Surface Conditions: Heavy bag marks, moderate abrasions, poor luster

Approximate Die Varieties: 3

Grade:	60	63	64	65	67	69	PL63	PL65
Approximate Availablity	1,290	460	115	40	5	1-2	70	25
Obtainability (Scale of 1 to 10)	7	8	8	9	10	10	8	9

Grade:	60-63	64	65	67-69	PL63	PL65
Investment Forecast: (percentage of return, annual simple interest)	10	10+	20	15-20	10	20

Investment Desirability by Grade:

MS - 60 MS - 64 MS - 67 MS - 63PL

MS - 63 MS - 65 MS - 69 MS - 65PL

Blue = Superior **Red = Excellent** **Green = Average** **Black = Below Average**

Note: Very few '93-Os appear, even when considering the extremely low mintage, in any grades. This coin falls in the middle of the '89 to '97 New Orleans poor strikes series. Locating a gem or prooflike gem could be nearly a lifetime project unless you are willing to set auction records in locating that particular gem for your set. This date is representative of the collector-type coin because most investors will not take the years required to search for that just right coin.

1893 S

Statistics

Mintage: 100,000 (lowest mintage of all business strike Morgans)

Fullness of Strike: Average S mint, many are very well struck

Normal Surface Conditions: Light to moderate bag marks, full luster, moderate abrasions

Approximate Die Varieties: 1

Grade:	60	63	64	65	67	69	PL63	PL65
Approximate Availablity	115	45	18	12	1-2	1-2	7	1-2
Obtainability (Scale of 1 to 10)	8	9	9	9	10	10	10	10

Grade:	60-63	64	65	67-69	PL63	PL65
Investment Forecast: (percentage of return, annual simple interest)	10+	10+	15	15	10-15	15

Investment Desirability by Grade:

MS - 60	MS - 64	MS - 67	MS - 63PL
MS - 63	MS - 65	MS - 69	MS - 65PL

Blue = Superior **Red = Excellent** **Green = Average** **Black = Below Average**

Note: Probably this is the most renowned date of the Morgan Series. This date had large numbers melted, as well as heavy circulation for most of the coins immediately. Again, a specially trained professional look may need to be taken when considering this date for an investment, because many altered coins are in the marketplace.

1893 CC

Statistics

Mintage: 677,000

Fullness of Strike: Majority are a notoriously poor strike (last year of CC and not too impressive for most cases of this year). Some full strikes do appear but are heavily bag marked.

Normal Surface Conditions: Average luster, moderate to heavy bag marks and abrasions

Approximate Die Varieties: 3

Grade:	60	63	64	65	67	69	PL63	PL65
Approximate Availablity	2,675	2,100	1,170	920	70	30	1,775	230
Obtainability (Scale of 1 to 10)	5	5	6	8	8	9	6	9

Grade:	60-63	64	65	67-69	PL63	PL65
Investment Forecast: (percentage of return, annual simple interest)	10	10+	15-20	15-20	10	15-20

Investment Desirability by Grade:

MS - 60	Black
MS - 63	Black
MS - 64	Black
MS - 65	Green
MS - 67	Green
MS - 69	Green
MS - 63PL	Black
MS - 65PL	Green

Blue = Superior **Red = Excellent** **Green = Average** **Black = Below Average**

Note: The last year the Carson City Mint was operational for Morgan Dollars. Similar to the '92-CC, these 1893-CC dollars were not held in the Treasury's hoard. The '93-CC is somewhat easy to locate in flat strikes with numerous abrasions, in uncirculated Mint State 60 to 63.

1894

Statistics

Mintage: 110,972 (Proof 972)

Fullness of Strike: Average, many pieces nicely struck considering the second lowest mintage of Morgan dollars

Normal Surface Conditions: Average P mint bag marks, moderate abrasions, average luster

Approximate Die Varieties: 1

Grade:	60	63	64	65	67	69	PL63	PL65
Approximate Availablity	1,700	810	565	330	100	45	60	34
Obtainability (Scale of 1 to 10)	5	6	7	8	8	9	8	10

Grade:	60-63	64	65	67-69	PL63	PL65
Investment Forecast: (percentage of return, annual simple interest)	10	10+	15-20	15-20	10+	15+

Investment Desirability by Grade:

Black: MS - 60	Black: MS - 64	Green: MS - 67	Green: MS - 63PL
Black: MS - 63	Green: MS - 65	Green: MS - 69	Red: MS - 65PL

Blue = Superior **Red = Excellent** **Green = Average** **Black = Below Average**

Note: This date has been widely notorious for altered coins. These have had mint marks removed from 1894 S and O mint dollars. Again, great caution should be used when buying this date, unless it is purchased from a highly reputable dealer. Many unsuspecting so-called expert investors later wish they had had their coin viewed by a trained eye before purchasing.

1894 O

Statistics

Mintage: 1,723,000

Fullness of Strike: Very poor, below average O mint, also a match to 1893-O in its poor quality

Normal Surface Conditions: Heavy bag marks and abrasions, very flat appearance, very poor luster

Approximate Die Varieties: 6

Grade:	60	63	64	65	67	69	PL63	PL65
Approximate Availablity	2,475	1,185	465	130	75	1-2	38	8
Obtainability (Scale of 1 to 10)	6	7	8	9	8	10	8	9

Grade:	60-63	64	65	67-69	PL63	PL65
Investment Forecast: (percentage of return, annual simple interest)	10+	10+	15+	20	20	20

Investment Desirability by Grade:

MS - 60	MS - 64	MS - 67	MS - 63PL
MS - 63	MS - 65	MS - 69	MS - 65PL

Blue = Superior **Red = Excellent** **Green = Average** **Black = Below Average**

Note: Again, another truly rare coin in uncirculated condition. The investor may wait a lifetime just to own one gem of this date. Very similar in characteristics of the 1889 through '97-O mint series. Unfortunately, like many scarce and elusive dates, they are being out performed by most of the common dates due to the huge popularity and large amount of coins that change hands in these more common dates. Less than a dozen '94-O Mint States 63 and better coins may change hands in a given year.

1894 S

Statistics

Mintage: 1,260,000

Fullness of Strike: Average S mint strike, majority full strikes

Normal Surface Conditions: Light to average bag marks, average luster, moderate to heavy abrasions

Approximate Die Varieties: 3

Grade:	60	63	64	65	67	69	PL63	PL65
Approximate Availablity	4,560	3,150	1,350	910	115	70	963	345
Obtainability (Scale of 1 to 10)	5	6	6	7	8	8	6	8

Grade:	60-63	64	65	67-69	PL63	PL65
Investment Forecast: (percentage of return, annual simple interest)	10+	10+	15-20	15-20	10+	15+

Investment Desirability by Grade:

MS - 60 MS - 64 MS - 67 MS - 63PL

MS - 63 MS - 65 MS - 69 MS - 65PL

Blue = Superior Red = Excellent Green = Average Black = Below Average

Note: This date, like many of the preceeding coins, had much more popularity in the 1970s and earlier with collectors than they do with today's modern investor of the 1980s. Rather than searching months to locate that particular gem for a set, today's investor many times would rather accumulate quantities of lesser rarities and have his or her money working in a numismatic market rather than leaving the money set in banks finally waiting for that once in a lifetime purchase.

1895

Statistics

Mintage: 12,880 (Proof 880)

Fullness of Strike: Proof striking — almost every coin virtually full strike

Normal Surface Conditions: Hairlines and many circulated proofs

Approximate Die Varieties: 1

Grade (proofs):	60	63	64	65	67	69
Approximate Availablity	115	238	205	110	62	17
Obtainability (Scale of 1 to 10)	5	4	4	6	6	7

Grade (proofs):	60-63	64	65	67-69
Investment Forecast: (percentage of return, annual simple interest)	5-10	5-10	10	10+

Investment Desirability by Grade (proofs):

MS - 60 **MS - 64** **MS - 67**

MS - 63 **MS - 65** **MS - 69**

Blue = Superior **Red = Excellent** **Green = Average** **Black = Below Average**

Note: Although this date has been represented as the King of the Morgans, it is relatively easy to locate. Only a couple of business strikes (non-proofs) have ever been reported to have surfaced. The A.N.A. Certification Service documented a business strike for the first time in 1974. Notation to its potential buyer, most major coin conventions and auctions will have at least one 1895 proof, therefore he or she should select a choice, no hairlines specimen for investment. Not a high investment yield coin.

1895 O

Statistics

Mintage: 450,000

Fullness of Strike: Average O mint, weak obverse and especially reverse breast feathers

Normal Surface Conditions: Heavy bag marks and abrasions, dull luster

Approximate Die Varieties: 3

Grade:	60	63	64	65	67	69	PL63	PL65
Approximate Availablity	1,075	480	160	70	25	8	75	8
Obtainability (Scale of 1 to 10)	6	7	7	8	8	10	8	10

Grade:	60-63	64	65	67-69	PL63	PL65
Investment Forecast: (percentage of return, annual simple interest)	10	10+	20	20	10+	20

Investment Desirability by Grade:

MS - 60 MS - 64 MS - 67 MS - 63PL

MS - 63 MS - 65 MS - 69 MS - 65PL

Blue = Superior **Red = Excellent** **Green = Average** **Black = Below Average**

Note: Another date that may have priced itself out of the market for most investors due to the fact that less than a handful of true Mint State 63 or better coins surface each year. The advanced investor/collector is a possible buyer for this coin in gem condition, but in reality an investor would be much better off to select a small quantity of quality common and semi-common dates.

1895 S

Statistics

Mintage: 400,000

Fullness of Strike: Average S mint - contrary to popular opinion, coins average strike; many almost uncircualted coins sold as MS-60

Normal Surface Conditions: Moderate to heavy bag marks, average luster, moderate abrasions

Approximate Die Varieties: 3

Grade:	**60**	**63**	**64**	**65**	**67**	**69**	**PL63**	**PL65**
Approximate Availablity	3,600	1,210	395	265	160	25	675	210
Obtainability (Scale of 1 to 10)	6	7	7	8	9	9	6	7

Grade:	**60-63**	**64**	**65**	**67-69**	**PL63**	**PL65**
Investment Forecast: (percentage of return, annual simple interest)	10	10+	15+	15	15	20

Investment Desirability by Grade:

MS - 60	MS - 64	MS - 67	MS - 63PL
MS - 63	MS - 65	MS - 69	MS - 65PL

Blue = Superior **Red = Excellent** **Green = Average** **Black = Below Average**

Note: The same information holds true for the '95-O as the '95-S. Truly advanced investor/collectors should try to obtain this type of rarity. The overall profit potential looks much greater for less expensive coins of high mint state quality.

1896

Statistics

Mintage: 9,976,762 (Proof 762)

Fullness of Strike: Majority full strikes

Normal Surface Conditions: Light to moderate bag marks, full luster, average abrasions

Approximate Die Varieties: 8

Grade:	**60**	**63**	**64**	**65**	**67**	**69**	**PL63**	**PL65**
Approximate Availablity	59,000	46,000	17,850	13,750	1,200	850	6,500	1,650
Obtainability (Scale of 1 to 10)	2	2	2	4	4	5	3	4

Grade:	**60-63**	**64**	**65**	**67-69**	**PL63**	**PL65**
Investment Forecast: (percentage of return, annual simple interest)	20	20	30	30	10+	25

Investment Desirability by Grade:

[red] **MS - 60**	[red] **MS - 64**	[blue] **MS - 67**	[black] **MS - 63PL**
[red] **MS - 63**	[blue] **MS - 65**	[blue] **MS - 69**	[red] **MS - 65PL**

Blue = Superior **Red = Excellent** **Green = Average** **Black = Below Average**

Note: The first of a three-year run of common Philadelphia mint dates. The 1896- to '98-P mints represent the opposite in quality as the predecessor group of 1890 to '94. The '96-P, whether in rolls or gem singles, if the past is reflective of the future, will receive tremendous profit.

1896 O

Statistics

Mintage: 4,900,000

Fullness of Strike: Far below average, very weak obverse and reverse high points

Normal Surface Conditions: Heavy abrasions and bag marks, dull luster, very unattractive

Approximate Die Varieties: 13

Grade:	**60**	**63**	**64**	**65**	**67**	**69**	**PL63**	**PL65**
Approximate Availablity	3,100	1,650	750	200	30	5	125	16
Obtainability (Scale of 1 to 10)	7	7	7	8	10	10	7	9

Grade:	**60-63**	**64**	**65**	**67-69**	**PL63**	**PL65**
Investment Forecast: (percentage of return, annual simple interest)	10	20	30	30	30	30

Investment Desirability by Grade:

MS - 60	Green
MS - 63	Green
MS - 64	Red
MS - 65	Blue
MS - 67	Blue
MS - 69	Blue
MS - 63PL	Blue
MS - 65PL	Blue

Blue = Superior **Red = Excellent** **Green = Average** **Black = Below Average**

Note: Two significant major varieties in mint marks exist: large and small O on reverse. It is a shame that this coin is not available to be traded; very minute quantities are traded each year. Therefore, like many other dates, the '96-O is seldom encountered in grades above Mint State 63. This date represents the next to last of the poor strikes of the 1889- to '97-O series.

1896 S

Statistics

Mintage: 5,000,000

Fullness of Strike: Below average for S mint, typical weak reverse and hair above ear on obverse

Normal Surface Conditions: Heavy bag marks, average luster, many abrasions

Approximate Die Varieties: 3

Grade:	60	63	64	65	67	69	PL63	PL65
Approximate Availablity	4,600	2,800	1,475	675	60	28	190	35
Obtainability (Scale of 1 to 10)	5	6	7	7	8	9	9	9

Grade:	60-63	64	65	67-69	PL63	PL65
Investment Forecast: (percentage of return, annual simple interest)	10	10+	20	20+	20+	25+

Investment Desirability by Grade:

MS - 60 MS - 64 MS - 67 MS - 63PL

MS - 63 MS - 65 MS - 69 MS - 65PL

Blue = Superior **Red = Excellent** **Green = Average** **Black = Below Average**

Note: A truly rare coin, although more sought after by date collectors than modern day investors. A scarce coin that is sure to bring enormous prices at auctions for that true gem coin.

1897

Statistics

Mintage: 2,822,731 (Proof 731)

Fullness of Strike: Average full strike P mint

Normal Surface Conditions: Moderate bag marks, average luster, minimum abrasions

Approximate Die Varieties: 6

Grade:	60	63	64	65	67	69	PL63	PL65
Approximate Availablity	36,000	21,000	10,000	5,600	800	420	3,800	790
Obtainability (Scale of 1 to 10)	2	2	3	7	7	7	4	7

Grade:	60-63	64	65	67-69	PL63	PL65
Investment Forecast: (percentage of return, annual simple interest)	20	20	30	30	15	30

Investment Desirability by Grade:

MS - 60 (Red)	MS - 64 (Red)	MS - 67 (Red)	MS - 63PL (Green)
MS - 63 (Red)	MS - 65 (Red)	MS - 69 (Red)	MS - 65PL (Red)

Blue = Superior **Red = Excellent** **Green = Average** **Black = Below Average**

Note: A very underrated common date in mint state 65 or better. Regarding mintages and availability, this is definitely a coin of great promise. Another area of common date that an investor should eagerly purchase in singles or quantities.

1897 O

Statistics

Mintage: 4,004,000

Fullness of Strike: Below average O mint

Normal Surface Conditions: Poor luster, moderate to heavy bag marks, heavy abrasions

Approximate Die Varieties: 6

Grade:	**60**	**63**	**64**	**65**	**67**	**69**	**PL63**	**PL65**
Approximate Availablity	6,200	3,600	725	120	45	10	75	25
Obtainability (Scale of 1 to 10)	5	6	7	8	9	9	8	9

Grade:	**60-63**	**64**	**65**	**67-69**	**PL63**	**PL65**
Investment Forecast: (percentage of return, annual simple interest)	10	15	20	20	15	20

Investment Desirability by Grade:

MS - 60	Black
MS - 63	Black
MS - 64	Green
MS - 65	Green
MS - 67	Green
MS - 69	Red
MS - 63PL	Green
MS - 65PL	Red

Blue = Superior **Red = Excellent** **Green = Average** **Black = Below Average**

Note: The last of the terrible O series of 1889- to '97-O mint. Again, this date is extremely elusive, and in many cases it is recommended to purchase lesser rarities in high quality, rather than waiting for a once in a lifetime gem purchase.

1897 S

Statistics

Mintage: 5,825,000

Fullness of Strike: Average S fullness, best strike of the late 1890s

Normal Surface Conditions: Moderate bag marks, average luster, heavy abrasions

Approximate Die Varieties: 7

Grade:	60	63	64	65	67	69	PL63	PL65
Approximate Availablity	37,000	11,000	7,000	3,000	755	250	8,000	1,500
Obtainability (Scale of 1 to 10)	3	3	3	4	5	8	4	4

Grade:	60-63	64	65	67-69	PL63	PL65
Investment Forecast: (percentage of return, annual simple interest)	10	10	20	20	10-15	20

Investment Desirability by Grade:

MS - 60 MS - 64 MS - 67 MS - 63PL

MS - 63 MS - 65 MS - 69 MS - 65PL

Blue = Superior Red = Excellent Green = Average Black = Below Average

Note: The '97-S has long been a promotional coin in grades of MS-60 to -63. Large quantities of true MS-65 or better have never been dispersed. Frequently found in small hoards, the '97-S is often overlooked by new investors believing that a promotional coin may have lost some merit in terms of purchase. This concept is incorrect, and true gems will be a steady producer of profit in years to come. True gems should not show the cloudy luster that is common for this date.

1898

Statistics

Mintage: 5,884,735 (Proof 735)

Fullness of Strike: Above average, many full strikes

Normal Surface Conditions: Light bag marks, full luster, moderate abrasions

Approximate Die Varieties: 4

Grade:	60	63	64	65	67	69	PL63	PL65
Approximate Availablity	96,000	85,000	35,000	11,000	1,500	900	2,600	1,600
Obtainability (Scale of 1 to 10)	2	3	3	4	6	7	4	5

Grade:	60-63	64	65	67-69	PL63	PL65
Investment Forecast: (percentage of return, annual simple interest)	20	20	35	30	20	30

Investment Desirability by Grade:

MS - 60 (Red)	MS - 64 (Blue)	MS - 67 (Red)	MS - 63PL (Green)
MS - 63 (Red)	MS - 65 (Blue)	MS - 69 (Red)	MS - 65PL (Red)

Blue = Superior **Red = Excellent** **Green = Average** **Black = Below Average**

Note: Very similar to the 1896 and '97 Philadelphia dates. This is especially true of the outlook for the '98, as it was the '97-P. True gems are underrated, and great profit will be had by the astute investor. An excellent short- or long-term investment in uncirculated Mint States grades.

1898 O

Statistics

Mintage: 4,440,000

Fullness of Strike: Majority are full strikes, although there are a small number of very flat, unattractive coins

Normal Surface Conditions: Light bag marks, full luster, moderate abrasions

Approximate Die Varieties: 12

Grade:	60	63	64	65	67	69	PL63	PL65
Approximate Availablity	208,000	201,000	101,000	23,500	3,100	990	5,700	2,300
Obtainability (Scale of 1 to 10)	2	2	2	4	6	7	4	4

Grade:	60-63	64	65	67-69	PL63	PL65
Investment Forecast: (percentage of return, annual simple interest)	20	20	35	30	20	30

Investment Desirability by Grade:

Color	Grade	Color	Grade	Color	Grade	Color	Grade
Red	MS - 60	Blue	MS - 64	Blue	MS - 67	Green	MS - 63PL
Red	MS - 63	Blue	MS - 65	Blue	MS - 69	Red	MS - 65PL

Blue = Superior **Red = Excellent** **Green = Average** **Black = Below Average**

Note: As mentioned previously, this is the third year in which an investor can purchase two different mints and both be of common price for the same year. This occurrance happens only once each decade, i.e. 1878-P & -S, 1885-P & -O, 1898-P & -O and 1900-P & -O. A very good investment date.

1898 S

Statistics

Mintage: 4,102,000

Fullness of Strike: Below average S mint, majority not fully struck

Normal Surface Conditions: Moderage bag marks, average S mint luster, heavy abrasions

Approximate Die Varieties: 6

Grade:	60	63	64	65	67	69	PL63	PL65
Approximate Availablity	11,000	3,000	2,700	1,200	400	150	1,700	775
Obtainability (Scale of 1 to 10)	4	4	5	6	7	7	5	7

Grade:	60-63	64	65	67-69	PL63	PL65
Investment Forecast: (percentage of return, annual simple interest)	10	10-15	20	20	10	20

Investment Desirability by Grade:

MS - 60 (Black) MS - 64 (Green) MS - 67 (Green) MS - 63PL (Black)

MS - 63 (Black) MS - 65 (Green) MS - 69 (Green) MS - 65PL (Green)

Blue = Superior **Red = Excellent** **Green = Average** **Black = Below Average**

Note: This date has been known to be found in small hoards from time to time. The '98-S has also been found in quantity in the Redfield Collection. Strict gems are difficult to locate, but with a little perseverance this date may be obtained.

1899

Statistics

Mintage: 330,846* (Proof 846)

Fullness of Strike: Average P mint, many specimens from this date are fully struck even with such a small mintage

Normal Surface Conditions: Moderate bag marks, full luster, many semi prooflike coins, average P mint abrasions

Approximate Die Varieties: 3

Grade:	60	63	64	65	67	69	PL63	PL65
Approximate Availablity	18,800	13,100	2,600	1,950	475	280	1,400	700
Obtainability (Scale of 1 to 10)	4	4	4	6	6	7	5	7

Grade:	60-63	64	65	67-69	PL63	PL65
Investment Forecast: (percentage of return, annual simple interest)	10	10+	20	20	15	20+

Investment Desirability by Grade:

MS - 60 MS - 64 MS - 67 MS - 63PL

MS - 63 MS - 65 MS - 69 MS - 65PL

Blue = Superior Red = Excellent Green = Average Black = Below Average

* Note: Author does not agree with mintage figures. This coin, even though somewhat a better date, has never been hard to locate in quantities in most grades. This date is not tremendously popular because of the controversy over the possible inaccuracies of total mintage figures among experts.

1899 O

Statistics

Mintage: 12,290,000

Fullness of Strike: Majority far above average strikes

Normal Surface Conditions: Full luster, light to moderate bag marks, minimum abrasions

Approximate Die Varieties: 15

Grade:	**60**	**63**	**64**	**65**	**67**	**69**	**PL63**	**PL65**
Approximate Availablity	113,000	166,000	41,000	19,000	2,200	450	3,950	1,650
Obtainability (Scale of 1 to 10)	2	2	2	4	5	6	4	5

Grade:	**60-63**	**64**	**65**	**67-69**	**PL63**	**PL65**
Investment Forecast: (percentage of return, annual simple interest)	20+	20+	30+	35+	20	35

Investment Desirability by Grade:

MS - 60 (Red)	MS - 64 (Red)	MS - 67 (Blue)	MS - 63PL (Green)
MS - 63 (Red)	MS - 65 (Blue)	MS - 69 (Blue)	MS - 65PL (Blue)

Blue = Superior **Red = Excellent** **Green = Average** **Black = Below Average**

Note: Profitability diagnosis is exceptionally strong for the future of this date. For many years it was considered another common New Orleans date, but Mint State 65 and better coins are now receiving a justifiable recognition as a very profitable area to invest.

1899 S

Statistics

Mintage: 2,562,000

Fullness of Strike: Above average, typical S mint strike

Normal Surface Conditions: Light to moderate bag marks, luster above average, heavy abrasions

Approximate Die Varieties: 10

Grade:	60	63	64	65	67	69	PL63	PL65
Approximate Availablity	3,750	2,940	925	785	425	275	1,700	495
Obtainability (Scale of 1 to 10)	4	6	6	7	8	8	7	8

Grade:	60-63	64	65	67-69	PL63	PL65
Investment Forecast: (percentage of return, annual simple interest)	10	15	20	20	15	20

Investment Desirability by Grade:

MS - 60	MS - 64	MS - 67	MS - 63PL
MS - 63	MS - 65	MS - 69	MS - 65PL

Blue = Superior **Red = Excellent** **Green = Average** **Black = Below Average**

Note: Although the 1899-S is somewhat difficult to locate, it is usually the easiest of the 1898 to 1904 S mint series, and the last date of the San Francisco Mint that can be located in gem quality with any immediate success. The large mintage distorts the availability of this particular date.

1900

Statistics

Mintage: 8,830,912 (Proof 912)

Fullness of Strike: Begins the poor strikes for 1900-01-02-04 P mints

Normal Surface Conditions: Moderate to heavy bag marks, average to below average luster, grey luster, moderate abrasions

Approximate Die Varieties: 11

Grade:	60	63	64	65	67	69	PL63	PL65
Approximate Availablity	91,000	39,500	18,000	5,100	675	315	2,300	975
Obtainability (Scale of 1 to 10)	4	4	5	6	7	8	6	7

Grade:	60-63	64	65	67-69	PL63	PL65
Investment Forecast: (percentage of return, annual simple interest)	20	20	35	35	20	30

Investment Desirability by Grade:

MS - 60 (Red)	MS - 64 (Red)	MS - 67 (Blue)	MS - 63PL (Green)
MS - 63 (Red)	MS - 65 (Blue)	MS - 69 (Blue)	MS - 65PL (Red)

Blue = Superior **Red = Excellent** **Green = Average** **Black = Below Average**

Note: With high mintages, and the normal large quantities of over worked dies, true Mint State 65 or better is a very promising coin. Like the 1878-P & -S, 1885-P & -O, and 1898-P & -O, the 1900-P & 1900-O can be accumulated in quantity and is the last year in which dollars can be collected in two mints in one year at common prices.

1900 O

Statistics

Mintage: 12,590,000

Fullness of Strike: Majority are poor to average strikes

Normal Surface Conditions: Heavy bag marks, better than average luster, heavy abrasions

Approximate Die Varieties: 26

Grade:	60	63	64	65	67	69	PL63	PL65
Approximate Availablity	147,000	121,000	39,000	11,500	1,900	475	4,100	2,050
Obtainability (Scale of 1 to 10)	2	2	3	4	6	7	5	5

Grade:	60-63	64	65	67-69	PL63	PL65
Investment Forecast: (percentage of return, annual simple interest)	20+	25	30	35	25	35

Investment Desirability by Grade:

MS - 60	MS - 64	MS - 67	MS - 63PL
MS - 63	MS - 65	MS - 69	MS - 65PL

Blue = Superior **Red = Excellent** **Green = Average** **Black = Below Average**

Note: Two major varieties for this date, 1900-O and 1900-O over CC. Presumably, a few old Carson City working dies were used later in New Orleans in unsuccessful attempts at retooling the mint marks on the working dies. This date as well as the 1900-P, represent more "sleepers," as the investors pour into the dollar market absorbing large amounts of what used to be *common* dollars.

1900 S

Statistics

Mintage: 3,540,000

Fullness of Strike: Majority have poor strikes, flat, non-attractive

Normal Surface Conditions: Average S mint luster, moderate to heavy bag marks

Approximate Die Varieties: 6

Grade:	60	63	64	65	67	69	PL63	PL65
Approximate Availablity	12,000	7,000	2,000	1,250	400	100	3,100	900
Obtainability (Scale of 1 to 10)	5	6	6	7	8	8	6	7

Grade:	60-63	64	65	67-69	PL63	PL65
Investment Forecast: (percentage of return, annual simple interest)	10	10-15	20	25+	20	20

Investment Desirability by Grade:

MS - 60	MS - 64	MS - 67	MS - 63PL
MS - 63	MS - 65	MS - 69	MS - 65PL

Blue = Superior **Red = Excellent** **Green = Average** **Black = Below Average**

Note: The 1900-S is a very difficult coin to locate with full strikes on both obverse and reverse. This date always seems to turn up in hoards (i.e., Redfield) and majority of the coins wll be heavily bag marked and abraded with many flat strikes. This is a characteristic that is uncommon to the San Francisco series with a mintage of over 3½ million.

1901

Statistics

Mintage: 6.962,813 (Proof 813)

Fullness of Strike: Very flat

Normal Surface Conditions: Heavy bag marks, far below average luster, light abrasions

Approximate Die Varieties: 4

Grade:	60	63	64	65	67	69	PL63	PL65
Approximate Availablity	1,400	265	115	35	5-6	1-2	17	4
Obtainability (Scale of 1 to 10)	6	7	8	9	10	10	9	10

Grade:	60-63	64	65	67-69	PL63	PL65
Investment Forecast: (percentage of return, annual simple interest)	10	15	25	30+	30+	40+

Investment Desirability by Grade:

MS - 60 MS - 64 MS - 67 MS - 63PL

MS - 63 MS - 65 MS - 69 MS - 65PL

Blue = Superior Red = Excellent Green = Average Black = Below Average

Note: The single most difficult Philadelphia date to obtain of all the Morgan series. Many collectors, after a lifetime of searching, have settled for an AU or MS-60 to -63 coin. Not a date recommended for the impatient investor with a small checkbook. This coin would be priced many times its value if there could be more pieces available for active trading between dealers.

1901 O

Statistics

Mintage: 13,320,000

Fullness of Strike: Very poor, many flat strikes

Normal Surface Conditions: Heavy bag marks, many heavy abrasions, below average luster

Approximate Die Varieties: 8

Grade:	60	63	64	65	67	69	PL63	PL65
Approximate Availablity	192,000	113,000	37,000	11,000	2,000	300	7,500	3,500
Obtainability (Scale of 1 to 10)	1	2	3	4	5	6	5	5

Grade:	60-63	64	65	67-69	PL63	PL65
Investment Forecast: (percentage of return, annual simple interest)	15	15	25+	25	20	25

Investment Desirability by Grade:

MS - 60 [green]	MS - 64 [green]	MS - 67 [red]	MS - 63PL [green]
MS - 63 [green]	MS - 65 [red]	MS - 69 [red]	MS - 65PL [red]

Blue = Superior **Red = Excellent** **Green = Average** **Black = Below Average**

Note: Many dealers and investors try to classify the '01-O as another common New Orleans mintage year. This is doing the '01-O a grave injustice. Finding superb coins can be a very difficult task, even in small amounts. In gem quality, the '01-O is a steadily rising date, and should be looked into as a year to invest in.

1901 S

Statistics

Mintage: 2,284,000

Fullness of Strike: Two major types, one exceptionally flat, one average S mint; both have weak reverses

Normal Surface Conditions: Moderate to heavy bag marks, below average luster

Approximate Die Varieties: 4

Grade:	**60**	**63**	**64**	**65**	**67**	**69**	**PL63**	**PL65**
Approximate Availablity	4,600	2,850	1,900	750	275	30	650	200
Obtainability (Scale of 1 to 10)	5	6	7	7	8	9	8	8

Grade:	**60-63**	**64**	**65**	**67-69**	**PL63**	**PL65**
Investment Forecast: (percentage of return, annual simple interest)	10	10	20	20	20	20

Investment Desirability by Grade:

MS - 60	**MS - 64**	**MS - 67**	**MS - 63PL**
MS - 63	**MS - 65**	**MS - 69**	**MS - 65PL**

Blue = Superior **Red = Excellent** **Green = Average** **Black = Below Average**

Note: This date is plagued with polished dies, creating many choice coins with heavy striations. To locate a gem example of this date free of striations is very hard. When buying this date don't be hasty to satisfy yourself with an inferior strike. Remember two major varieties exist, and full strikes on both obverse and reverse do exist.

1902

Statistics

Mintage: 7,994,777 (Proof 777)

Fullness of Strike: Below average for P mint; reverse normally weaker than obverse.

Normal Surface Conditions: Typical late P mint with grey-colored surfaces, average luster and bag marks, moderate abrasions

Approximate Die Varieties: 3

Grade:	**60**	**63**	**64**	**65**	**67**	**69**	**PL63**	**PL65**
Approximate Availablity	11,000	4,000	2,500	1,475	500	190	1,350	450
Obtainability (Scale of 1 to 10)	4	4	5	6	8	8	7	7

Grade:	**60-63**	**64**	**65**	**67-69**	**PL63**	**PL65**
Investment Forecast: (percentage of return, annual simple interest)	10	15+	20	20	20	30

Investment Desirability by Grade:

■ MS - 60 (Black)	■ MS - 64 (Green)	■ MS - 67 (Green)	■ MS - 63PL (Green)
■ MS - 63 (Black)	■ MS - 65 (Green)	■ MS - 69 (Green)	■ MS - 65PL (Red)

Blue = Superior **Red = Excellent** **Green = Average** **Black = Below Average**

Note: Contrary to popular belief, many more than expected prooflike coins have changed hands, not all having the typical grey surfaces. This date has turned up in small hoards with remarkably good luster and true prooflike surfaces. The future for this date is very positive, and profitable.

1902 O

Statistics

Mintage: 8,636,000

Fullness of Strike: From 1898 to 1904, probably the weakest strike, usually flat struck

Normal Surface Conditions: Heavy bag marks, many abrasions, below average luster

Approximate Die Varieties: 10

Grade:	60	63	64	65	67	69	PL63	PL65
Approximate Availablity	168,000	129,000	33,750	9,500	1,775	400	4,320	1,875
Obtainability (Scale of 1 to 10)	1	3	3	4	5	7	4	6

Grade:	60-63	64	65	67-69	PL63	PL65
Investment Forecast: (percentage of return, annual simple interest)	20+	20	35	30	20	25

Investment Desirability by Grade:

MS - 60 MS - 64 MS - 67 MS - 63PL

MS - 63 MS - 65 MS - 69 MS - 65PL

Blue = Superior Red = Excellent Green = Average Black = Below Average

Note: Many characteristics are the same as the early New Orleans Series; large quantities of flat strikes and multiple abrasions and bag marks do exist. Huge profit potentials are prevalent in this date. Possibly overlooked by many as a typical poor strike coin, Mint State 65 and better will receive great support from buyers in the next few years.

1902 S

Statistics

Mintage: 1,530,000

Fullness of Strike: Below average for S mint, many light strikes, very weak reverse, very difficult to find fully struck with no striations

Normal Surface Conditions: Most often found with striations, below average S mint luster, moderate bag marks

Approximate Die Varieties: 4

Grade:	**60**	**63**	**64**	**65**	**67**	**69**	**PL63**	**PL65**
Approximate Availablity	5,700	1,725	1,100	675	175	60	400	205
Obtainability (Scale of 1 to 10)	5	6	6	7	8	9	9	9

Grade:	**60-63**	**64**	**65**	**67-69**	**PL63**	**PL65**
Investment Forecast: (percentage of return, annual simple interest)	10	15	20	30	30	30

Investment Desirability by Grade:

MS - 60 **MS - 64** **MS - 67** **MS - 63PL**

MS - 63 **MS - 65** **MS - 69** **MS - 65PL**

Blue = Superior **Red = Excellent** **Green = Average** **Black = Below Average**

Note: Probably one of the dates with the heaviest striations. Not the full brilliance of an S mint as compared to an early year S mint dollar. Finding an MS-65 or better without the striations is next to impossible. Not highly looked upon as an investment date in less than MS-65.

1903

Statistics

Mintage: 4,652,755 (Proof 755)

Fullness of Strike: Average and better than most P mints, similar to 1883-'87-P mints in strike characteristics

Normal Surface Conditions: Grey luster, many lustrous pieces confused for semi prooflike. Average bag marks with moderate abrasions.

Approximate Die Varieties: 3

Grade:	60	63	64	65	67	69	PL63	PL65
Approximate Availablity	26,000	18,000	15,000	4,000	1,800	400	2,500	800
Obtainability (Scale of 1 to 10)	3	3	3	3	4	6	5	6

Grade:	60-63	64	65	67-69	PL63	PL65
Investment Forecast: (percentage of return, annual simple interest)	10	10-15	20	15-20	15	20

Investment Desirability by Grade:

■ MS - 60	■ MS - 64	■ MS - 67	■ MS - 63PL
■ MS - 63	■ MS - 65	■ MS - 69	■ MS - 65PL

(MS-60, MS-63: Black; MS-64, MS-65, MS-67, MS-69, MS-63PL, MS-65PL: Green)

Blue = Superior **Red = Excellent** **Green = Average** **Black = Below Average**

Note: Surprisingly large numbers of this date survived in uncirculated grades. This date's availability is similar to the 1899-P. Although luster is very different between the two dates, each date commands a better than common price, yet can be easily located.

1903 O

Statistics

Mintage: 4,450,000

Fullness of Strike: Once again, another below average O mint

Normal Surface Conditions: Heavy bag marks, very average luster, many abrasions

Approximate Die Varieties: 3

Grade:	60	63	64	65	67	69	PL63	PL65
Approximate Availablity	28,000	22,000	11,000	3,000	750	250	1,650	1,100
Obtainability (Scale of 1 to 10)	3	3	4	5	5	6	5	6

Grade:	60-63	64	65	67-69	PL63	PL65
Investment Forecast: (percentage of return, annual simple interest)	10-15	15	20	20	20	30

Investment Desirability by Grade:

MS - 60 MS - 64 MS - 67 MS - 63PL

MS - 63 MS - 65 MS - 69 MS - 65PL

Blue = Superior Red = Excellent Green = Average Black = Below Average

Note: A very large surplus of this date has been present since its large release in 1962. Many collectors will remember its popularity during the 1960s, until the release of so many pieces. This date is much scarcer in circulated grades than in Mint State 60 or better.

1903 S

Statistics

Mintage: 1,241,000

Fullness of Strike: Above average, typical for S mint

Normal Surface Conditions: Light to moderate bag marks, excellent luster, moderate abrasions

Approximate Die Varieties: 3

Grade:	60	63	64	65	67	69	PL63	PL65
Approximate Availablity	2,300	1,475	875	520	105	25	300	315
Obtainability (Scale of 1 to 10)	6	7	8	8	9	9	9	9

Grade:	60-63	64	65	67-69	PL63	PL65
Investment Forecast: (percentage of return, annual simple interest)	10+	10+	15	20+	20+	25+

Investment Desirability by Grade:

MS - 60	MS - 64	MS - 67	MS - 63PL
MS - 63	MS - 65	MS - 69	MS - 65PL

Blue = Superior **Red = Excellent** **Green = Average** **Black = Below Average**

Note: A very rare coin, but not that many pieces exist to change hands, therefore often overlooked. Truly a key to collecting a complete set, but modern investors are turning away from elusive expensive dates and accumulating quantities of quality common dates.

1904

Statistics

Mintage: 2,788,650 (Proof 650)

Fullness of Strike: Like the 1901-P, very weak, in the top five dates for P mint flatness

Normal Surface Conditions: Heavy bag marks, frequent abrasions, dull luster, often grey in color

Approximate Die Varieties: 3

Grade:	**60**	**63**	**64**	**65**	**67**	**69**	**PL63**	**PL65**
Approximate Availablity	24,700	4,300	2,000	980	285	70	700	175
Obtainability (Scale of 1 to 10)	4	5	6	8	8	8	8	9

Grade:	**60-63**	**64**	**65**	**67-69**	**PL63**	**PL65**
Investment Forecast: (percentage of return, annual simple interest)	10	10-15	15-20	25	20	35

Investment Desirability by Grade:

MS - 60 **MS - 64** **MS - 67** **MS - 63PL**

MS - 63 **MS - 65** **MS - 69** **MS - 65PL**

Blue = Superior **Red = Excellent** **Green = Average** **Black = Below Average**

Note: Even though this coin is difficult to locate in high grades, this date is not very popular. The 1904-P has had a tremendous price upsurge and many investors are not willing to pay the new price for a gem.

1904 O

Statistics

Mintage: 3,720,000

Fullness of Strike: Another typical O mint; two major varieties, one exceptionally flat, one average

Normal Surface Conditions: Heavy bag marks, many abrasions, full luster

Approximate Die Varieties: 10

Grade:	60	63	64	65	67	69	PL63	PL65
Approximate Availablity	405,000	360,000	48,000	28,000	2,000	1,000	6,000	2,000
Obtainability (Scale of 1 to 10)	1	2	2	3	6	7	4	5

Grade:	60-63	64	65	67-69	PL63	PL65
Investment Forecast: (percentage of return, annual simple interest)	20+	20+	30	30	20	30

Investment Desirability by Grade:

MS - 60	MS - 64	MS - 67	MS - 63PL
MS - 63	MS - 65	MS - 69	MS - 65PL

Blue = Superior **Red = Excellent** **Green = Average** **Black = Below Average**

Note: The last New Orleans dated coin for Morgan dollars. A truly unique example of another date that may be overlooked by new investors while the wise investor is accumulating as many as can be located of these common date prices.

1904 S

Statistics

Mintage: 2,304,000

Fullness of Strike: Below average for an S mint, weak reverse breast feathers

Normal Surface Conditions: Moderate to heavy bag marks, average luster, heavy abrasions

Approximate Die Varieties: 1

Grade:	**60**	**63**	**64**	**65**	**67**	**69**	**PL63**	**PL65**
Approximate Availablity	6,000	3,000	1,800	850	375	45	150	30
Obtainability (Scale of 1 to 10)	6	7	7	8	9	9	9	9

Grade:	**60-63**	**64**	**65**	**67-69**	**PL63**	**PL65**
Investment Forecast: (percentage of return, annual simple interest)	15	15-20	30	35	30	40

Investment Desirability by Grade:

MS - 60 MS - 64 MS - 67 MS - 63PL

MS - 63 MS - 65 MS - 69 MS - 65PL

Blue = Superior **Red = Excellent** **Green = Average** **Black = Below Average**

Note: The last of the difficult 1898- to '04-S mint expensive coins. As stated previously, many of the exceptionally higher priced coins in MS-65 are being passed over by the less patient investor who wants money invested immediately. A truly scarce coin in Mint State 65 or better.

1921

Statistics

Mintage: 44,690,000

Fullness of Strike: For as many coins produced, many soft strikes, some above average strikes exist

Normal Surface Conditions: Medium to heavy bag marks, many lackluster coins, average to heavy abrasions

Approximate Die Varieties: 6

Grade:	60	63	64	65	67	69	PL63	PL65
Approximate Availablity	4,618,000	358,000	48,500	17,500	4,000	2,000	12,000	2,500
Obtainability (Scale of 1 to 10)	1	2	2	4	6	6	6	6

Grade:	60-63	64	65	67-69	PL63	PL65
Investment Forecast: (percentage of return, annual simple interest)	20	25	30	30	20	30

Investment Desirability by Grade:

MS - 60 MS - 64 MS - 67 MS - 63PL

MS - 63 MS - 65 MS - 69 MS - 65PL

Blue = Superior Red = Excellent Green = Average Black = Below Average

Note: The 1921-P represents the most common of all Morgans in Mint State 60. This fact doesn't hold true in MS-65 and better. An average '21 is not a glamorous coin. It has large potential in all mint state grades because of the availability to be promoted by many dealers at the same time.

1921 D

Statistics

Mintage: 20,345,000

Fullness of Strike: Very weak, flatness on obverse and reverse

Normal Surface Conditions: Heavy bag marks, less than average luster, heavy abrasions

Approximate Die Varieties: 3

Grade:	60	63	64	65	67	69	PL63	PL65
Approximate Availablity	49,500	17,000	5,000	2,750	650	300	700	200
Obtainability (Scale of 1 to 10)	3	3	4	6	8	7	8	9

Grade:	60-63	64	65	67-69	PL63	PL65
Investment Forecast: (percentage of return, annual simple interest)	10	15	20-25	30	20	30

Investment Desirability by Grade:

MS - 60 MS - 64 MS - 67 MS - 63PL

MS - 63 MS - 65 MS - 69 MS - 65PL

Blue = Superior **Red = Excellent** **Green = Average** **Black = Below Average**

Note: The 1921-D is the only date of the Morgan series that has a Denver mint mark. This coin receives very little popularity in MS-60 to -64 grades, but in Mint State 65 or better is very sought after by many dealers and investors.

1921 S

Statistics

Mintage: 21,695,000

Fullness of Strike: Very weak, flat obverse and reverse

Normal Surface Conditions: Heavy bag marks, less than average luster

Approximate Die Varieties: 2

Grade:	60	63	64	65	67	69	PL63	PL65
Approximate Availablity	54,000	7,500	4,000	1,500	250	35	1,375	175
Obtainability (Scale of 1 to 10)	2	3	4	6	7	9	6	9

Grade:	60-63	64	65	67-69	PL63	PL65
Investment Forecast: (percentage of return, annual simple interest)	10	10-15	20-25	30+	10-15	35

Investment Desirability by Grade:

MS - 60　MS - 64　MS - 67　MS - 63PL

MS - 63　MS - 65　MS - 69　MS - 65PL

Blue = Superior　Red = Excellent　Green = Average　Black = Below Average

Note: Finding quantities of Mint State 60s is not difficult. The task of finding gem is very much the same as with the 1921-D; very difficult. Probably one of the harder coins in the Morgan series for many people to grade. This is the last date of the remarkable Morgan series.

PEACE SILVER DOLLARS

SPECIFICATIONS

DESIGNER:	Anthony De Francisci
WEIGHT:	26.73 grams
COMPOSITION:	.900 silver, .100 copper
DIAMETER:	38.1 mm.
MINTS:	Philadelphia, Denver, San Francisco
NET WEIGHT:	.77344 oz. pure silver

1921

Statistics

Mintage: 1,006,473

Fullness of Strike: Two major die varieties, one exceptionally weak, one above average

Normal Surface Conditions: Average bag marks, below average luster

Approximate Die Varieties: 2

Grade:	**60**	**63**	**64**	**65**	**67**	**69**
Approximate Availablity	16,500	12,250	1,800	1,000	360	205
Obtainability (Scale of 1 to 10)	4	4	5	5	6	7

Grade:	**60-63**	**64**	**65**	**67-69**
Investment Forecast: (percentage of return, annual simple interest)	10	15	20	20

Investment Desirability by Grade:

MS - 60	Black
MS - 63	Black
MS - 64	Black
MS - 65	Black
MS - 67	Green
MS - 69	Green

Blue = Superior **Red = Excellent** **Green = Average** **Black = Below Average**

Note: The 1921 Peace Dollar, when in true gem condition, is the finest looking of all Peace dollars. Because of the high relief of the first year, the complete depth and design details cannot be equalled. Many 1921 are sold each year as gems, when in reality very few fully struck MS-65 or better coins trade hands.

1922

Statistics

Mintage: 51,737,000

Fullness of Strike: Majority full strikes, beginning of nice strikes P mint Peace dollars

Normal Surface Conditions: Light to moderate bag marks, full luster, minimum abrasions

Approximate Die Varieties: 3

Grade:	60	63	64	65	67	69
Approximate Availablity	3,245,000	2,837,000	373,000	27,500	4,000	1,350
Obtainability (Scale of 1 to 10)	1	1	2	3	4	5

Grade:	60-63	64	65	67-69
Investment Forecast: (percentage of return, annual simple interest)	15+	20+	30+	35+

Investment Desirability by Grade:

(Green) MS - 60	(Red) MS - 64	(Blue) MS - 67
(Red) MS - 63	(Blue) MS - 65	(Blue) MS - 69

Blue = Superior **Red = Excellent** **Green = Average** **Black = Below Average**

Note: Along with the 1923-P, these two dates are considered to be the most common of all the Peace dollars. Struck in very large numbers, these two dates allow many investors the opportunity to select many MS-65 and better coins for their investment portfolios. This date, like the 1923-P, has a great potential for profit, especially due to the large popularity of locating extremely nice specimens, much the same as the 1881-S Morgan dollar.

1922 D

Statistics

Mintage: 15,063,000

Fullness of Strike: Average

Normal Surface Conditions: Average bag marks, medium to below average luster

Approximate Die Varieties: 1

Grade:	60	63	64	65	67	69
Approximate Availablity	18,000	6,500	3,750	1,100	375	120
Obtainability (Scale of 1 to 10)	2	3	4	5	7	8

Grade:	60-63	64	65	67-69
Investment Forecast: (percentage of return, annual simple interest)	10-15	15	20	25+

Investment Desirability by Grade:

MS - 60	Black
MS - 63	Black
MS - 64	Black
MS - 65	Green
MS - 67	Green
MS - 69	Green

Blue = Superior **Red = Excellent** **Green = Average** **Black = Below Average**

Note: This is the Denver Mint's first entry into the Peace dollar series. Coins produced at this mint totalled only five years production (1922, '23, '26, '27 and '34) and are considered to fall into group "B" of overall obtainability. Group A consists of the Philadelphia struck dates with their much bolder strike; then Denver with much weaker strikes overall, and last the San Francisco dates, which are seldom encountered in any quantity of bold strikes.

1922 S

Statistics

Mintage: 17,475,000

Fullness of Strike: Very weak obverse and reverse, flat, unattractive

Normal Surface Conditions: Heavy bag marks, many abrasions, below average luster, first of the 1922-28 poor, visually displeasing S mint strikes

Approximate Die Varieties: 1

Grade:	60	63	64	65	67	69
Approximate Availablity	43,000	14,000	11,100	415	42	15
Obtainability (Scale of 1 to 10)	2	3	5	7	8	9

Grade:	60-63	64	65	67-69
Investment Forecast: (percentage of return, annual simple interest)	10	10-15	20	20-25

Investment Desirability by Grade:

MS - 60 MS - 64 MS - 67

MS - 63 MS - 65 MS - 69

Blue = Superior **Red = Excellent** **Green = Average** **Black = Below Average**

Note: The normal 1922-S is an exceptionally weak strike, and many investors for this reason have passed over most San Francisco Mint Peace dollars. Selecting a gem of any of the 1922 to '28 S mint dollars is going to be a major task. Many investors as well as dealers are always willing to pay astronomical prices for gem 1922-S through 1928-S dollars, with very few ever having to part with their money.

1923

Statistics

Mintage: 30,800,000

Fullness of Strike: Exceptionally full, majority are far above average "P" mint Peace

Normal Surface Conditions: Light bag marks, full luster, light to moderate abrasions

Approximate Die Varieties: 5

Grade:	**60**	**63**	**64**	**65**	**67**	**69**
Approximate Availablity	2,250,000	1,650,000	275,000	34,000	5,750	1,250
Obtainability (Scale of 1 to 10)	1	1	1	1	1	1

Grade:	**60-63**	**64**	**65**	**67-69**
Investment Forecast: (percentage of return, annual simple interest)	15+	20+	30+	35+

Investment Desirability by Grade:

MS - 60 (Green) **MS - 64** (Red) **MS - 67** (Blue)

MS - 63 (Red) **MS - 65** (Blue) **MS - 69** (Blue)

Blue = Superior **Red = Excellent** **Green = Average** **Black = Below Average**

Note: As mentioned with the 1922-P dollar, the '23-P is equally as common in quantity available and profit potential in years to come. Since these two dates receive large amounts of volume trading each year, they are very well liked by dealers as well as investors, and are very easy to liquidate at any time.

1923 D

Statistics

Mintage: 6,811,000

Fullness of Strike: Average for D mint

Normal Surface Conditions: Moderate to average bag marks, full luster, moderate to heavy abrasions

Approximate Die Varieties: 4

Grade:	**60**	**63**	**64**	**65**	**67**	**69**
Approximate Availablity	65,000	12,000	4,000	3,500	1,200	600
Obtainability (Scale of 1 to 10)	2	3	4	6	6	6

Grade:	**60-63**	**64**	**65**	**67-69**
Investment Forecast: (percentage of return, annual simple interest)	10	20	20	20-25

Investment Desirability by Grade:

MS - 60

MS - 63

MS - 64

MS - 65

MS - 67

MS - 69

Blue = Superior **Red = Excellent** **Green = Average** **Black = Below Average**

Note: A 1923-D dollar represents the second year of Denver Peace dollars, and is considered to be average strike, above the quality received by the '22-D. The only date that is fuller struck and more attractive than the '23-D is the 1926-D, the best appearing of all Denver Peace dollars. Don't misunderstand and think that '23-Ds are exceptionally easy to locate; their whereabouts are not common knowledge to many.

1923 S

Statistics

Mintage: 19,020,000

Fullness of Strike: Exceptionally weak, very flat

Normal Surface Conditions: Heavy bag marks, lackluster, below average; another average "S" mint for 1922-28 strikes.

Approximate Die Varieties: 3

Grade:	60	63	64	65	67	69
Approximate Availablity	42,000	17,000	1,200	310	45	8
Obtainability (Scale of 1 to 10)	2	3	5	8	8	9

Grade:	60-63	64	65	67-69
Investment Forecast: (percentage of return, annual simple interest)	10	10+	20	35+

Investment Desirability by Grade:

MS - 60 (Black)
MS - 63 (Black)
MS - 64 (Black)
MS - 65 (Green)
MS - 67 (Blue)
MS - 69 (Blue)

Blue = Superior **Red = Excellent** **Green = Average** **Black = Below Average**

Note: With regards to average strike versus gems available, the 1923-S is probably the hardest coin to find in Mint State 65 or better. Years may go by before a true gem is ever offered at auction. If a fully struck '23-S is a coin that you set your sights on owning, patience and record-breaking purchase price will be needed to complete the transaction.

1924

Statistics

Mintage: 11,811,000

Fullness of Strike: Excellent, majority full strikes

Normal Surface Conditions: Light bag marks, full luster, minimum abrasions

Approximate Die Varieties: 2

Grade:	60	63	64	65	67	69
Approximate Availablity	196,000	188,000	102,000	14,000	2,500	1,175
Obtainability (Scale of 1 to 10)	2	2	2	3	6	7

Grade:	60-63	64	65	67-69
Investment Forecast: (percentage of return, annual simple interest)	20	20+	30	30

Investment Desirability by Grade:

Green	MS - 60
Red	MS - 63
Red	MS - 64
Blue	MS - 65
Blue	MS - 67
Blue	MS - 69

Blue = Superior **Red = Excellent** **Green = Average** **Black = Below Average**

Note: Many dealers and investors alike refer to the 1924-P and '25-P as common dates as well. This is a little deceiving because Mint State 65 coins command multiples of the '22 to '23 Philadelphia sister dates. A strong potential gain can be achieved by this date and many astute investors are stocking up as many gems as they can locate.

1924 S

Statistics

Mintage: 1,728,000

Fullness of Strike: Very weak, obverse and reverse exceptionally flat

Normal Surface Conditions: Very flat, dull, below average luster, heavy bag marks, moderate to heavy abrasions

Approximate Die Varieties: 1

Grade:	60	63	64	65	67	69
Approximate Availablity	17,000	5,000	1,420	750	75	20
Obtainability (Scale of 1 to 10)	3	4	6	7	8	9

Grade:	60-63	64	65	67-69
Investment Forecast: (percentage of return, annual simple interest)	10	10+	20	25

Investment Desirability by Grade:

MS - 60   MS - 64   MS - 67

MS - 63   MS - 65   MS - 69

Blue = Superior   **Red = Excellent**   **Green = Average**   **Black = Below Average**

Note: Another of the very difficult and almost impossible fully struck S mint dates in the Peace dollar series. Many investors either purchase Mint State 60 to 64, or pass the date completely because of their impatience at not being able to locate a choice example immediately. This date has had numerous promotions in the quality of Mint State 60 to 63. There has never been, in recent years, a large hoard of Mint State 65 examples.

1925

Statistics

Mintage: 10,198,000

Fullness of Strike: Excellent, majority full strikes

Normal Surface Conditions: Light bag marks, full luster, light abrasions

Approximate Die Varieties: 1

Grade:	60	63	64	65	67	69
Approximate Availablity	185,000	139,000	76,000	5,000	2,000	1,000
Obtainability (Scale of 1 to 10)	2	2	3	3	3	3

Grade:	60-63	64	65	67-69
Investment Forecast: (percentage of return, annual simple interest)	15+	20	35	35

Investment Desirability by Grade:

MS - 60   MS - 64   MS - 67

MS - 63   MS - 65   MS - 69

Blue = Superior   **Red = Excellent**   **Green = Average**   **Black = Below Average**

Note: Similar to the 1924-P, this date has almost exactly the same characteristics as well as price per grade. The '24-P may have a little more popularity, but the appearance and profit potential is still very equal. Many gem examples as well as choice rolls do exist and investors should not hesitate to acquire large amounts for years to come.

1925 S

Statistics

Mintage: 1,610,000

Fullness of Strike: Very weak, another S mint Peace flat strike

Normal Surface Conditions: Heavy bag marks, below average luster, heavy abrasions

Approximate Die Varieties: 1

Grade:	60	63	64	65	67	69
Approximate Availablity	29,000	13,000	1,000	440	53	15
Obtainability (Scale of 1 to 10)	4	5	7	8	9	9

Grade:	60-63	64	65	67-69
Investment Forecast: (percentage of return, annual simple interest)	10	10+	20	25

Investment Desirability by Grade:

MS - 60 (Black)	MS - 64 (Black)	MS - 67 (Red)
MS - 63 (Black)	MS - 65 (Green)	MS - 69 (Red)

Blue = Superior **Red = Excellent** **Green = Average** **Black = Below Average**

Note: Again another San Francisco strike that is not on a par with the Philadelphia strike of the same date. Selecting a gem S mint in Peace dollars in recent years may have turned out to be very rewarding if the time spent searching revealed one at most any price.

1926

Statistics

Mintage: 1,939,000

Fullness of Strike: Full, another P mint productivity

Normal Surface Conditions: Minimum to average bag marks, full luster, moderate abrasions

Approximate Die Varieties: 1

Grade:	60	63	64	65	67	69
Approximate Availablity	38,000	28,000	5,000	3,000	1,000	500
Obtainability (Scale of 1 to 10)	3	3	4	5	5	5

Grade:	60-63	64	65	67-69
Investment Forecast: (percentage of return, annual simple interest)	10-15	20	25	30+

Investment Desirability by Grade:

MS - 60	**MS - 64**	**MS - 67**
MS - 63	**MS - 65**	**MS - 69**

Blue = Superior **Red = Excellent** **Green = Average** **Black = Below Average**

Note: In regards to investment potential, the 1926-P is starting to set standards that will be very hard to equal. Once considered slightly better than the common date Peace dollars, its price is now worthy of many multiples of the common date Peace dollars, 1922- to '23-P. Full luster and strike gems await the investor, and so do large profits in the near future.

1926 D

Statistics

Mintage: 2,348,700

Fullness of Strike: Fullest "D" mint Peace Dollar

Normal Surface Conditions: Full luster, light bag marks, above average Peace dollar

Approximate Die Varieties: 1

Grade:	**60**	**63**	**64**	**65**	**67**	**69**
Approximate Availablity	138,000	24,000	9,000	4,000	800	250
Obtainability (Scale of 1 to 10)	3	3	3	6	7	7

Grade:	**60-63**	**64**	**65**	**67-69**
Investment Forecast: (percentage of return, annual simple interest)	10+	15+	20	30+

Investment Desirability by Grade:

MS - 60 MS - 64 MS - 67

MS - 63 MS - 65 MS - 69

Blue = Superior **Red = Excellent** **Green = Average** **Black = Below Average**

Note: Representing the fullest strike of the Denver Mint Peace dollars the 1926-D would be everyones'choice. Many gems carry that golden color usually found on 1925-P dollars. This particular date is receiving many investor's attention, and is surely a profitable date in the near future.

1926 S

Statistics

Mintage: 6,980,000

Fullness of Strike: Third fullest S mint Peace dollar, still many weak strikes available

Normal Surface Conditions: Moderate to heavy bag marks, full luster, average abrasions

Approximate Die Varieties: 2

Grade:	60	63	64	65	67	69
Approximate Availablity	25,000	15,000	5,000	3,000	460	215
Obtainability (Scale of 1 to 10)	4	4	5	5	8	8

Grade:	60-63	64	65	67-69
Investment Forecast: (percentage of return, annual simple interest)	10	15	25	30

Investment Desirability by Grade:

MS - 60 (Black)
MS - 63 (Black)
MS - 64 (Green)
MS - 65 (Red)
MS - 67 (Red)
MS - 69 (Red)

Blue = Superior **Red = Excellent** **Green = Average** **Black = Below Average**

Note: Following the 1922 to '25 San Francisco dates, finally a small ray of hope emerged with a minute amount of full strike '26-S dollars available. By no means is it possible to accumulate quantities like the common '22 and '23 Philadelphia coins, but it is a pleasant change from some of the previous drab S mint Peace dollars. This year is particularly important because without purchasing the more expensive '27, '28, '34 and '35 S mints, this date represents the only full strike available for a modest price. A popular coin.

1927

Statistics

Mintage: 848,000

Fullness of Strike: Average P mint, majority are full strikes

Normal Surface Conditions: Light to moderate bag marks, full luster, light abrasions

Approximate Die Varieties: 1

Grade:	**60**	**63**	**64**	**65**	**67**	**69**
Approximate Availablity	8,000	4,100	3,000	1,270	270	128
Obtainability (Scale of 1 to 10)	4	4	5	6	6	6

Grade:	**60-63**	**64**	**65**	**67-69**
Investment Forecast: (percentage of return, annual simple interest)	10-15	15	30	35+

Investment Desirability by Grade:

Blue = Superior **Red = Excellent** **Green = Average** **Black = Below Average**

Note: With regards to rarity, the 1927-P is much more difficult to find than the '26-P. Although this date has been overlooked in lower Mint State grades 60 to 64 by many collectors and investors, prosperity is sure to happen for the Mint State 65 and better coins. Small amounts are known to exist with very full luster, but they have unusual quantities of very small bag marks on the obverse and reverse.

1927 D

Statistics

Mintage: 1,268,900

Fullness of Strike: Average with many full strikes

Normal Surface Conditions: Moderate bag marks, average to above average luster, minimum abrasions

Approximate Die Varieties: 1

Grade:	60	63	64	65	67	69
Approximate Availablity	15,000	10,000	3,000	2,000	660	300
Obtainability (Scale of 1 to 10)	3	3	4	6	6	7

Grade:	60-63	64	65	67-69
Investment Forecast: (percentage of return, annual simple interest)	10	10-15	20	30

Investment Desirability by Grade:

MS - 60 (Black)　MS - 64 (Green)　MS - 67 (Red)

MS - 63 (Black)　MS - 65 (Green)　MS - 69 (Red)

Blue = Superior　**Red = Excellent**　**Green = Average**　**Black = Below Average**

Note: A coin that still can be found in small hoards or pockets around the country. This date received much more popularity in the 1970's than in the 1980's. True gems have been dispersed in larger quantities than novice dealers believe to be possible. Extremely large hoards of '23-D, '26-D, and '27-D have been known to exist in bag quantities (many pieces are heavily bag marked and even large amount of sliders were in the bags).

1927 S

Statistics

Mintage: 866,000

Fullness of Strike: Very weak

Normal Surface Conditions: Heavy bag marks, below average luster, heavy abrasions

Approximate Die Varieties: 2

Grade:	60	63	64	65	67	69
Approximate Availablity	5,800	1,850	500	365	100	20
Obtainability (Scale of 1 to 10)	5	6	7	8	9	9

Grade:	60-63	64	65	67-69
Investment Forecast: (percentage of return, annual simple interest)	10	10-15	20	25

Investment Desirability by Grade:

MS - 60 (Black)   MS - 64 (Green)   MS - 67 (Red)

MS - 63 (Black)   MS - 65 (Green)   MS - 69 (Red)

Blue = Superior **Red = Excellent** **Green = Average** **Black = Below Average**

Note: Next to last year of below average weak strike S mints. This particular coin has suffered for years with lack of popularity in Mint State 65 or better. Never have large quantities of gems ever been released on the marketplace in recent years. Truly a difficult coin to locate and, unfortunately there are many coins that have more promising futures than the '27-S with regards to profit.

1928

Statistics

Mintage: 360,649

Fullness of Strike: Average

Normal Surface Conditions: Light to moderate bag marks, average luster, minimum to moderate abrasions

Approximate Die Varieties: 1

Grade:	60	63	64	65	67	69
Approximate Availablity	9,000	2,700	2,500	1,900	500	250
Obtainability (Scale of 1 to 10)	3	3	4	4	4	4

Grade:	60-63	64	65	67-69
Investment Forecast: (percentage of return, annual simple interest)	10	10-15	15	20+

Investment Desirability by Grade:

MS - 60   MS - 64   MS - 67

MS - 63   MS - 65   MS - 69

Blue = Superior   **Red = Excellent**   **Green = Average**   **Black = Below Average**

Note: A very deceiving coin because of its very low total mintage. Unfortunately, it is never a hard task to locate the '28-P. At almost every major show or auction many pieces can be readily purchased. This fact is true in acquiring singles only. At only one major show in the last few years there have been many small hoards released (1981 ANA New Orleans). Possibly slightly over performed by its reputation, rather than its profitability.

1928 S

Statistics

Mintage: 1,632,000

Fullness of Strike: Extremely weak

Normal Surface Conditions: Heavy bag marks, below average luster, many abrasions

Approximate Die Varieties: 1

Grade:	60	63	64	65	67	69
Approximate Availablity	7,975	2,320	1,350	450	115	12
Obtainability (Scale of 1 to 10)	4	4	5	8	8	9

Grade:	60-63	64	65	67-69
Investment Forecast:	10	10+	25	30-35

(percentage of return, annual simple interest)

Investment Desirability by Grade:

MS - 60	**MS - 64**	**MS - 67**
MS - 63	**MS - 65**	**MS - 69**

Blue = Superior **Red = Excellent** **Green = Average** **Black = Below Average**

Note: Last year of the flat and less desirable San Francisco dollars (1922-28). Thankfully, the flat characteristics did not carry through to the 1934 and 1935 San Francisco Mint dollars. The '28-S can in many ways compare to the '27-S. Truly a difficult coin to locate in gem quality.

1934

Statistics

Mintage: 954,057

Fullness of Strike: Average, majority full strikes

Normal Surface Conditions: Minimum bag marks, moderate abrasions, full luster

Approximate Die Varieties: 1

Grade:	60	63	64	65	67	69
Approximate Availablity	13,000	7,500	4,000	1,950	680	250
Obtainability (Scale of 1 to 10)	3	3	4	5	6	7

Grade:	60-63	64	65	67-69
Investment Forecast: (percentage of return, annual simple interest)	10	15-20	3C	30

Investment Desirability by Grade:

MS - 60	MS - 64	MS - 67
MS - 63	MS - 65	MS - 69

Blue = Superior **Red = Excellent** **Green = Average** **Black = Below Average**

Note: A very attractive coin to the investor is the '34-P. This date meets most of the criteria that .t takes to be a profitable purchase. A 1934-P dollar is a very well-liked coin among dealers and investors alike, whether buying or selling. Excluding the common dates, the '34-P is probably one of the better struck Peace dollars of the series.

1934 D

Statistics

Mintage: 1,569,500

Fullness of Strike: Weak, some amounts of full strikes do exist

Normal Surface Conditions: Heavy bag marks, average luster, moderate abrasions

Approximate Die Varieties: 2

Grade:	**60**	**63**	**64**	**65**	**67**	**69**
Approximate Availablity	15,000	3,000	1,360	660	180	50
Obtainability (Scale of 1 to 10)	4	4	5	7	8	8

Grade:	**60-63**	**64**	**65**	**67-69**
Investment Forecast: (percentage of return, annual simple interest)	10	10-15	30	30+

Investment Desirability by Grade:

MS - 60 **MS - 64** **MS - 67**

MS - 63 **MS - 65** **MS - 69**

Blue = Superior **Red = Excellent** **Green = Average** **Black = Below Average**

Note: A gem Mint State 65 or better 1934-D is a difficult date to locate. This date, which recently has had very small amounts sold on the marketplace, has become very elusive to investors. Majority of pieces found will have numerous bag marks but the overall look of the coin is somewhat pleasing, having nice full luster throughout the date run.

1934 S

Statistics

Mintage: 1,011,000

Fullness of Strike: Above average for S mint Peace dollar

Normal Surface Conditions: Above average, full luster, average bag marks, minimum abrasions

Approximate Die Varieties: 2

Grade:	60	63	64	65	67	69
Approximate Availablity	2,430	1,370	985	710	160	54
Obtainability (Scale of 1 to 10)	5	5	5	5	6	7

Grade:	60-63	64	65	67-69
Investment Forecast: (percentage of return, annual simple interest)	10	15	20	20+

Investment Desirability by Grade:

MS - 60　　MS - 64　　MS - 67

MS - 63　　MS - 65　　MS - 69

Blue = Superior　　**Red = Excellent**　　**Green = Average**　　**Black = Below Average**

Note: The "key" to the Peace dollar series in degree of price, not rarity of strike. There are many Peace dollars that have much worse strikes and are many times more difficult to locate. Locating a gem '34-S is by no means exceptionally easy, but the coin can be purchased at most major auctions and coin conventions throughout the year.

1935

Statistics

Mintage: 1,576,000

Fullness of Strike: Excellent strikes

Normal Surface Conditions: Minimum bag marks, full luster, light abrasions

Approximate Die Varieties: 1

Grade:	60	63	64	65	67	69
Approximate Availablity	25,000	17,000	8,800	3,000	970	470
Obtainability (Scale of 1 to 10)	4	5	5	5	6	7

Grade:	60-63	64	65	67-69
Investment Forecast: (percentage of return, annual simple interest)	10	10-15	25	30+

Investment Desirability by Grade:

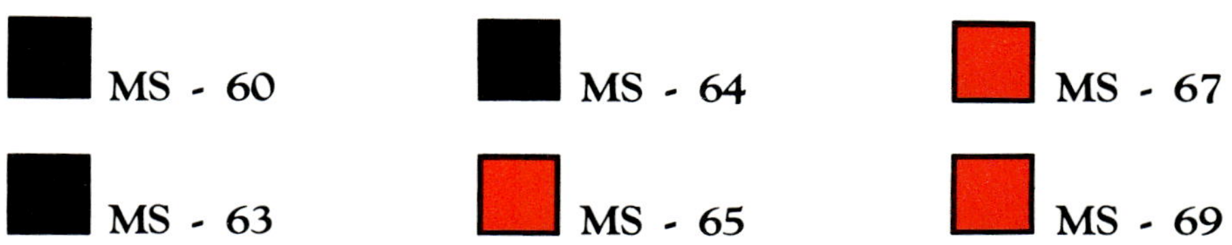

Blue = Superior **Red = Excellent** **Green = Average** **Black = Below Average**

Note: Last of the Philadelphia series Peace dollars. The '35-P is like the '34-P in being a popular and profitable coin to invest in. Many dealers and investors alike feel it will be a short time before the '35-P is selling for more than the '27-P. A coin to watch in the future.

1935 S

Statistics

Mintage: 1,964,000

Fullness of Strike: Soft, some weakness on reverse eagle feathers

Normal Surface Conditions: Very lustrous, moderate bag marks, probably second easiest S mint to locate in full strike

Approximate Die Varieties: 4

Grade:	60	63	64	65	67	69
Approximate Availablity	19,000	8,000	1,200	810	70	35
Obtainability (Scale of 1 to 10)	4	5	6	7	8	8

Grade:	60-63	64	65	67-69
Investment Forecast: (percentage of return, annual simple interest)	10	10-15	20	30+

Investment Desirability by Grade:

MS - 60 | MS - 64 | MS - 67

MS - 63 | MS - 65 | MS - 69

Blue = Superior **Red = Excellent** **Green = Average** **Black = Below Average**

Note: Completing the entire series of Peace dollars is the '35-S. A very lusterous coin that occasionally can be found with a pleasing full strike and many people bidding for the same coin. The '26-S and '35-S are about the same in many characteristics: i.e. one of the few years San Francisco produced fuller strikes than normal; it is virtually impossible to locate large quantities in gem condition; and finally, it is apparently twice as difficult to locate and is priced accordingly.

7

A SUCCESSFUL STRATEGY FOR INVESTING IN SILVER DOLLARS

For more than 15 years, this author has been actively involved in investing in rare, gem-quality silver dollars. This successful long-term investment activity has led to the development of some basic principles regarding silver dollar investments, which are offered in this chapter.

In essence, the key concepts relating to investing successfully in silver dollars can be broken down into five major areas: the quality of the coins involved; the convenience of silver dollars in terms of buying and selling the coins that will comprise the investment portfolio; the flexibility of silver dollars as an investment medium; the reputation, or "track record" of the dealer involved in selecting "winning" programs; and the dual considerations of the term of the investment required for full maturity, and the return on investment that can realistically be estimated in advance.

Quality: This is a key area in terms of my own experience in silver dollar investing. Extensive research has demonstrated that the best silver dollars for investment purposes are those that grade MS-65, which are also known as "gem-quality, brilliant uncirculated" coins. This is due in large measure to one of the basics of all economic considerations: supply and demand. (*Special note:* The average quantity of MS-65 coins in a given year's production is less than five percent. This is not to say that each date offers five percent of its total production in MS-65 condition; this is an average.)

It is also important to note that this grade is recommended for individual coin purchases with the utmost quality in mind. Some successful investors prefer to buy rolls or bags (1,000 coins) of MS-60 to MS-64 quality coins. This method is based on the fact that MS-65 coins are rarely available in enough quantity to be sold as rolls (20 coins) or in bags.

The U.S. Mints no longer produce any Morgan or Peace silver dollars. Indeed, they stopped producing silver dollars in 1935 (with the temporary, and undistributed, exception of the 1964 production. As noted earlier, these coins were all ordered melted down by the Director of the Mint in the same year they were produced). Since the available supply of these dollars declines each year for a wide variety of reasons (new investor purchases, past melting policies such as the 1918 Pittman Act, loss, theft, divorce, and donations to institutions), and since an increasing number of investors have become involved in purchasing these silver dollars, it follows that the value of these coins will continue to increase steadily.

This is the actual case: silver dollar investments have historically established a continuing upward "stair-step" pattern of increasing values. This stair-step pattern means that the appreciation in value of silver dollars has always continued in an upward direction. Major advances in the value of silver dollars have been preceeded and followed by periods called "plateaus." During these periods, the prices of silver dollars remains somewhat constant (as an overall rule; individual coins *do* continue to appreciate even during plateaus). Remember, that the silver dollars being discussed here are MS-65 pieces. Prices for lesser grades of silver dollars are much more affected by the fluctuations in the economy, rises and falls in the prime rate, the swings of prices in the silver bullion market, and other considerations. MS-65 silver dollars continue to increase in value, with little respect for what else is happening in the economy.

To review, an MS-65 silver dollar is one which is sharply struck, and has a very minimum of bagmarks and other abrasions on its fields and devices. It also has original luster or light toning. For Morgan dollars, the hair around the ears on the obverse is complete and the eagle on the reverse has sharply struck breast feathers; for the Peace series, the hair that covers the ears on the obverse is sharply struck, and the diagonal eagle feathers on the reverse are sharply struck. Again, roughly five percent of the silver dollars existing today fall into the MS-65 category. (For a complete review of each year and Mint's production, see Chapter 6.)

Convenience: This is another important aspect of investments in silver dollars. (A key factor in any investment is the ability to *buy* and *sell* the items involved. This meaning should be recognized throughout this discussion of silver dollar investing as a crucial difference between these and other investment media).

Since the coins involved are individually of high value, they can be stored easily in a private depository or safety deposit box. This makes them an inconspicuous investment that also offers a very high degree of immediate liquidity. Since silver dollars are always in high demand, they are easy to convert to cash, or to use in other financial transactions that will be discussed in the following section.

Flexibility: Coins have a wide range of available uses for the astute investor. They are obviously a lucrative form of generating personal wealth, but they also offer other uses as well. One of these is use as a trading medium.

Over the years, coins have been used to trade for luxury automobiles, mansions and luxury homes, real estate and development property, other tangibles such as gems and bullion, and even yachts. In addition, they may be used to transfer family wealth from one generation to the next, and coins can provide excellent collateral for securing loans.

Similarly, coins offer an individual the opportunity to develop tax credits when they are used as donations to non-profit institutions which have a functional use for them. An example of this is Metro Coin's assistance in donations to major universities on behalf of its clients. In these programs, coins are sold to an individual or firm, held for the minimum required time period, and then donated to a non-profit institution that meets the requirements of the tax laws.

Flexibility is also enhanced with silver dollar investments since coins can be sold, donated or traded either in individual lots, rolls of 20 coins, or in bags of 1,000 coins. This enables the owner to divide the coin portfolio as required to meet his or her own needs, without damaging the value of the remaining pieces.

Track Record: The track record of the professional who will be selecting the silver dollars is another important and basic consideration. The professional numismatist that is selected to handle your investment program should have a proven record of experience and dependability;

he should beware of trends in our industry (trends; not fads. This is a very important distinction as outlined in Chapter 8); he should offer investors an avenue for repurchase; and he should be a person in whom the investor can have confidence. A list of key questions to ask yourself about any potential numismatic investment program and numismatic firm is provided at the end of this chapter.

Term and Return on Investment: The final area is actually two considerations that are so interconnected that it is difficult to separate them. These are the term required for the investment to reach full maturity; and the return that can rationally be projected from silver dollar investments.

The *average* term of investment required to reach maturity in silver dollars is between three and five years. The range is neccessary here since each silver dollar investment has its own particular term to maturity, depending on a number of variables such as purchase price, condition of the particular coin or coins involved, the number of coins produced at that Mint during that given year, and the position of the silver dollar market at that moment in time in relation to the "stair step" pattern of appreciation described earlier in this chapter. Ideally, three to five years is a reasonable time in which one may expect the value of a particular coin to double, as a *minimum appreciation.* (This doubling in value is what I refer to as "maturity." Also, remember that this entire discussion is based on MS-65 grade coins).

Naturally many coins mature faster. Some coins that I have recommended in my monthly newsletter, *Update*, in the January issue of each year, have reported very impressive appreciation rates: some years have independently averaged an increase of more than 600 percent per year over a decade-long term of investment (simple interest). This demonstrates one of the key considerations involving silver dollar investment term: the longer a person holds the investment, generally speaking, the higher the return will be. Three to five years, as stated above, is a usual *minimum* term.

It should be obvious by now that silver dollar investments are not for the investor who wishes to buy today and sell back tomorrow. What silver dollars offer is a steady, medium- to long-term means of investing that returns excellent profits to the patient, steady, intelligent investor.

For example, if you had followed my recommendations, published in each January's issue of *Update* for the last decade, and had purchased $100,000 worth of the ten different silver dollars each January, for a decade-long investment of $1 million, my firm would buy those same recommended coins back today for a total price of more than $16 million. Remember, this total includes two years of coins (recommended dollars) which have yet to achieve maturity. This example also assumes that the coins have remained in the same condition in which they were purchased. These statistics have been verified by Metro Coin Ltd.'s Certified Public Accountant.

The personal recommendations published in *Update* are a service to my clients and *Update* subscribers, and are reviewed each year to determine the rate of return for each coin involved. If you are interested in a subscription, they are available through Metro Coin, Ltd. of Phoenix.

Questions to Ask A Numismatist Before Investing: The following is a list of basic questions that a potential silver dollar investor should ask a professional numismatist prior to commiting his or her funds to a transaction.

Some of these questions may not pertain to your particular situation, but there are very sound reasons behind each one, so the investor should be careful to weigh the answers the professional numismatist provides.

1. Are you a full-service numismatist? (Do you provide a repurchase policy; publish a monthly newsletter to keep your clients abreast of trends and movement in the industry; offer appraisals of existing pieces in a client's portfolio; insist on personal owner-client interaction or will I be shunted off to a commissioned staff member; do you stock a supply of the silver dollars you recommend on hand in your company's inventory, or do you have to order them from another dealer?) Remember, if the company you're dealing with has a high volume of transactions, delays in deliveries can occur. This does not reflect on the state or contents of the company's inventory, but rather on the back-log of order fulfilment; an important distinction.

2. What is your track record on recommendations? Recognizing the need to protect clients' confidentiality, what rate of return (or range of rates of return) have you generated for your clients' portfolios over the years?

3. Do you utilize the latest in state-of-the-art support systems such as teletype, computerization of records and inventory, and other technology? (This can also be used to determine the level of astuteness of the numismatist).

4. Are you a member of professional associations in the numismatic industry?

5. Are you a market-maker, or a market-follower? (Do you actively participate in generating transactions, as well as receiving them? Or do you simply report activity from the sidelines?)

6. How long has your firm been in business? (Does the operation look like it will still be in business in three to five years when your investment matures, should you seek to liquidate your portfolio?)

7. Does the numismatist explain all of the options involved in silver dollar investments? Does he take the time to explain the basics, and make certain that all of your questions are answered completely, or is he viewing you as a one-time sale?

8. Is the dealer making money himself from his own recommended investments?

9. What mark-up do you place on the coins you sell to investors? (The importance of this question is due to the wide range of responses that are possible within the numismatic industry. Some numismatists mark their products up more than 100 percent; others, who leave the bulk of the potential profit for the investor, mark up their coins between 10 and 20 percent, with the ideal being closer to 10 percent).

10. Is the dealer someone you will continue to enjoy doing business with over the years?

Obviously, not all of these questions *must* be asked of a potential numismatic advisor, but at least an indication of the answers to these questions is required to make an objective decision about who will select your silver dollar investments. Referrals are a good source of much of this information in most other industries. Unfortunately, that is not entirely the case in the numismatic field: since personal investments are confidential, clients rarely discuss their portfolios and profits with another potential investor. Unless you are already personally know someone who is doing business with a particular numismatist, it is unlikely that you will be able to get a direct reference. Even if you do get a personal referral, it is a good idea to ask these questions anyway.

A list of professional numismatists nationwide is provided in Chapter 9. You will note that the list is short, but that is so because these professionals have all been able to answer the questions above.

How Silver Dollar Investments Compare with Bullion Investments: A topic of considerable interest to investors, and rightfully so, is how silver dollar investments compare with other forms of investing, particularly with silver and gold bullion.

As most investors know, simply from reading the economic pages of their local newspaper, the prices of silver and gold bullion fluctuate randomly. In a given period, the per ounce rate may go up or down catastrophically. This leads to uncertainty and an element of "gambling with your nestegg" regarding bullion investment.

As an example of how silver dollar investments (based on my recommendations at the beginning of each year as described above) compare with silver and gold bullion, the bar graph on page 39 offers the listed prices for gold and silver on the first day of market trading for each year of the past decade. It also provides the price listed for my recommended coins on that same day of each year. This graph is a potent argument in favor of silver dollar investing in MS-65 grade, and has been a key factor in many clients' decision to begin a silver dollar portfolio.

Please Note: These comparison figures per year are not cumulative. Each year's recommendations stand on their own merits.

8

MYTHS AND THEORIES ABOUT COIN INVESTING

Even though coin collecting and professional numismatics has a relatively short past history, there are a number of myths and theories about this industry already in existance. Many of these are incorrect, and action by an investor based on some of these myths and theories can adversely effect his or her return on investment.

This chapter is designed to review some of these myths and theories; to point out potential pitfalls for the investors inherent in these concepts; and share some of this author's theories about the ideal and actual operation of the coin industry. Obviously, there are many more stories, "tall tales," and myths than can be reviewed in any one book, especially when one considers the connection that coins and minting in general have with the history of our nation. However, the myths and theories outlined here are intended to serve as a starting place for an examination of the "lore" of coin collecting and numismatics, and to whet the reader's appetite for more information and discussion.

Myth #1: Shinier is better.

This idea is based on a misunderstanding of grading principles. In grading, the basic criterion for determining the value of a coin is its appearance, and how its current appearance relates to that coin's mint state condition. This means that the Mint State system applies a number grade to a particular coin based on the quantity of bagmarks and other abrasions, scratches, wear, and marks on the coin. Original luster is also a consideration when grading uncirculated coins, and can make the difference of several grades.

However, the shininess of a coin is rarely a factor in the grading. Of course, there are exceptions: one is proof-like dollars which have shiny surfaces due to the condition of the dies when they were minted. Even in this case, though, the shininess can be a two-edged sword: it can make the coin look better, and thereby increase the coin's value; or, it can make the marks on the coin more pronounced, thereby lowering its value.

Indeed, some investors are willing to pay a premium for coins that are "toned," or slightly colored due to aging. Toning occurs in nearly every color of the rainbow, from brown to violet, and some coins even have a rainbow-like effect of several colors. As a result of this demand, toned coins are often valued more highly than their shinier cousins.

Theory #1: You Can Increase The Value of Your Coin By Polishing!

This theory is *totally incorrect!*

In fact, the only thing you can do to a coin by polishing it is to completely ruin its value. No professional numismatist will pay more than the value of the melted metal for a coin that has been polished.

As noted above, the value of a coin is determined by how nearly it matches its original condition when minted. Obviously then, polishing completely alters the surfaces of the coin, completely eliminates original luster, and attempts to mask imperfections. Polishing is also one way that an unscrupulous coin dealer might use to attempt to fool an unwary investor, and in this way charge a high price for a coin of much less value. *The Way To Avoid This Problem Is To Never Buy A Polished Coin At Any Price* (no matter how good a deal it seems at the time). If in doubt about whether a coin has been polished or not, ask the seller. More will be discussed later in this chapter on the subject of cleaning coins.

Myth #2: A Coin Only Has Two Sides.

For years, silver dollars have been represented as having only an obverse and reverse. However, coins actually have three sides; the third being the rim. This is particularly important in silver dollars, since the reeding on the rim is often a clue as to the true condition of the coin. If the rim is heavily nicked, cut, and abraded it is more than likely a MS-50 to -63 grade. A true gem MS-65 or better coin *will not* have major damage on the rim. (The reeding is laced on the coin by a collar die *before* the front and back are stamped). In cases in which a coin falls between two grades, the clues provided by the reeding can sometimes swing the balance of grading up or down one whole Mint State grading point.

Theory #2: It Is Possible For An Extremely Wealthy Person Or Group To Control The Silver Dollar Industry.

In theory this is hypothetically extremely possible; however, the realities of the coin industry make it unlikely.

Consider these factors: silver dollars are geographically spread from one end of the nation to the other, and the ownership varies from institutions (some of which are unable to sell their collections, even if they wish to, because of the terms under which they accepted them), to private individuals. Another factor is the extremely diverse nature of the coin industry itself: there are thousands of coin dealers in this country, all with inventory of their own and investors that they assist. These factors make it unlikely that any one individual, or group of individuals, could manipulate the coin industry in the way that other commodities have been manipulated in the past.

With the available technology, it is possible to ascertain the location of many coins. Knowing the number and coins in institutional collections, and subtracting them from the overall approximate supply, makes it easier to locate the remaining available pieces. At this point, once the coins have been located, price should be the only variable remaining.

Myth #3: A Coin Referred To As "Common" Is A "Below Average" Investment.

This myth is interesting in that it overlooks one of the basic principles of the coin industry: each coin should be judged on its own merits, in terms of the relative supply and demand it involves.

Another consideration is how the coin will fare in terms of return on investment over the next few years. This consideration is a combination of the coin's purchase price in a given condition in the current market, the term the investor is willing to hold the coin, and the relative position in the marketplace of that coin (is it currently undervalued or overvalued, for example). A coin that represents a year and mint with a high mintage may still be rare in a particular grade. Or, it may simply have better investment potential over the long run than a much more expensive coin.

It is also possible for a particular coin to be highly valued by an individual investor for some personal reason (the birthdate of a relative or ancestor, for example), or because it is the last coin required to complete a personal project such as a date-mint set.

Again, the best way to judge a coin is by examining its individual merits and then determining its relative position in the marketplace. This is sometimes a complicated process and often requires the assistance of a professional numismatist.

Theory #3: I Can Go To Coin Conventions and Auctions Myself and Save A Commission Fee.

A coin convention or auction is a gathering of a number of professional numismatists, coin dealers and collectors, and is not a very good place to learn the basics of numismatics, for what should be obvious reasons.

A beginning investor is much better advised to use a professional numismatist as an agent to obtain high-quality, investment grade coins, at least until he or she feels 100 percent confident with the many variables involved in this industry. There are several reasons for this. First, a coin convention or auction is a busy, active environment, not suited to one's best concentration. Second, lighting in the buildings in which these functions are held varies considerably; in some cases, the variations in lighting from convention hall to professionally-lighted examination room can result in as much as a whole grade point of difference. A whole grade point has a considerable impact on the value of the individual coin, as discussed in the chapters above.

In summary, it is not a good idea for a beginner to compete with an expert in any field, especially in a situation that involves as many variables of grade, type, mintmark, date, and condition as the coin industry.

Myth #4: There are 1964 Peace silver dollars in existance.

There is no sure way of either proving or disproving this story. As noted in Chapter 3, the U.S. Mint in Denver produced a large number of Peace silver dollars dated 1964. However, these coins were "ordered" destroyed by the Director of the Bureau of the Mint before they could be distributed for use as coinage.

Stories vary, of course, regarding the 1964 D Peace dollars. Some "old-timers" claim they have seen them, but only in informal settings; it would be tantamount to admitting to being an accessory after the fact in a felony to admit formally that one had even seen one of these coins, much less owned one. This is because it would have been necessary for someone to steal the coin in order to remove it from the Denver Mint after the Director of the Bureau of the Mint ordered them destroyed.

Theory #4: By the Year 2000, There Will Be No More Original Bags of B.U. Dollars Left.

Based on the current volume of sales of brilliant, uncirculated silver dollars in the United States and around the world, and the projections for increased sales in the years to come, it is very likely that all of the original bags will have been subdivided into 20-coin rolls and single coins by the year 2000.

The chart on Page 180 graphically demonstrates this author's estimate of the point at which supply will fall below demand.

Myth #5: A "Part Time" Or "Vest Pocket" Dealer Is The Equivalent Of A Professional Numismatist.

A "part time" or "vest pocket" dealer is *not* the equivalent of a professional numismatist, for a variety of reasons.

The dealer who is a part time or vest pocket dealer usually sells coins at prices and grades established by others (or at grades at which he or she *guesses*), and buys them in the same way. Often this is a side line to another business. As a rule, these dealers have a very low overhead, and do not extend into many areas of the coin industry. In many instances vest pocket dealers handle only coins that may be split grade (meaning the obverse or reverse is not matched). This allows the vest pocket dealer to sell his coins to less knowledgeable clients at the higher value of the two sides. Often, low overhead can be an advantage to the investor, but in this case, it is to be read more as a sign of the relative size of the dealer's operations. A dealer who *guesses* at values, or does not determine them himself, should not be trusted with an investor's nestegg.

On the other hand, a professional numismatist, as outlined in Chapter 9, has years of experience in buying and selling coins, and in grading them himself on the basis of accepted industry standards. In addition, a professional numismatist will deal in a much wider range of coins, as a rule, than a vest pocket dealer, even if he specializes in a particular type of coin.

The coin industry remains in the formative stages of establishing industry-wide standards of grading and pricing, but recent endeavors by individual professional numismatists and numismatic associations lead this author to be hopeful that more standards will be established in the very near future. While associations attempt to provide this type of guidelines, most do not have the enforcement capability necessary to make these standards effective without the voluntary cooperation of numismatists.

Theory #5: More and More Legislation Is Planned To Regulate the Numismatic Industry.

In the past 15 years of this author's experience in the coin industry, legislation has increasingly been enacted with the intent of regulating or restricting this industry.

This legislation has included changes in the income tax laws that restrict the use of rare coins (and other collectibles) in pension funds, I.R.A.s and Keogh plans; proposed restrictions on importing of certain coins, and the use of coins as tax-deductible donations. Regulation and red tape have historically found their way into any popular investment industry, and this author's belief is that the coin industry will be no exception to this general rule: as more and more investors become involved in the coin industry, there will naturally be more interest in our industry on the part of legislators.

Myth #6: Grading Will Eventually Return To Adjective Descriptions.

This is another totally false myth, in this author's opinion. The former system of grading (described in Chapter 4) simply is inadequate to describe the coin industry's needs today. In addition, the trend in grading is moving *away from* descriptive adjectives, and *toward* the use of more definite and exact Mint State numbers, as outlined in the Grading chapter of this book.

More and more, today's investors seek an exact, standardized system of grading from the coin industry. An investor who buys a silver dollar as MS-65 grade in one state wants to be able to sell it in that same grade (assuming it remains undamaged), even if he or she should move to another state. This is not always possible today, but it is my hope that it will be completely standardized at some near date.

Theory #6: The Numismatic Industry Will Eventually Involve Registration And Certification.

Like other industries involved with investor dollars, the coin industry has experienced an influx of unscrupulous dealers who wish to take advantage of this industry's popularity as an investment vehicle. As with other industries that have experienced this same trend in the past, such as commodities, stocks and real estate, the coin industry faces the choice of self-regulation or outside regulation. It is this author's hope and intent that our industry will move voluntarily in the direction of self-regulation, registration and certification; rather than have these same restrictions imposed from outside by the government.

Myth #7: All Morgan Silver Dollars Widely Fluctuate In An Overall Pattern.

This untrue myth assumes that all coins in a series fluctuate in value together. This is not always the case.

For example, in some instances, coin newsletter price lists will show a fluctuation in value from one weekly issue to the next for a coin that is so rare that no transactions involving that coin have taken place each and every week. In other words, some extremely rare coins are so few in number that it is possible to keep track of almost all of them. In this circumstance, it is possible to tell when a publication has inadvertently, or intentionally, altered the value listed even if no major auction or newly discovered rarity has come onto the marketplace.

The point is that all silver dollars have an independent market value. Each coin must be evaluated in terms of its quality, condition, popularity, availabilty, mintage and other factors, independent of all others.

Theory #7: Various Ideas About Buying Silver Dollars.

There are a number of ideas about buying silver dollars which fall under more or less the same heading: these involve the opportunities for special purchases which arise from time to time in our industry.

First, some people hesitate when confronted with an opportunity to buy a desired coin, even though it is correctly priced at the time. Much of this hesitation is due to the hope (vain, in most cases) that the "price will be cheaper later." Actually, the opposite is usually true. For whatever reason, and there is a wide range of them, certain coins are offered occasionally at prices which make them very attractive. When an investor sees a coin he or she feels is desirable at a fair price, it is a good idea to buy it then, rather than wait. As noted above, coins have historically increased in value. Therefore, if you see a coin you like, and it fits your investment plan (both in terms of desirability and price), purchase it immediately.

Second, many new investors are reluctant to buy a small "hoard" of exceptional coins when offered as a group. Often this reluctance is based upon a fear that buying a group of similar coins, even at a good price, will somehow reduce the value of the individual coins.

This is not the case. In terms of very high quality coins, quantity rarely drives prices down; indeed, it very often has the opposite effect and stimulates interest in these coins, thereby driving values up.

Third, opportunities arise occasionally in the coin industry to obtain high quality coins at favorable rates for reasons which have nothing to do with the actual value of the coins themselves.

For example, professional numismatists realize that many collections and portfolios are liquidated under adverse conditions. These include divorce, death, dissolution of partnerships, taxes, bankruptcies, etc., etc., etc. As a result, groups of coins become available for purchase at irregular intervals, often at very favorable prices due to the time restrictions involved in their immediate liquidation.

In spite of the relative urgency of these liquidations, however, one should not expect to "steal" these coins; this rarely happens. What very often *does* happen, though, is that the coins are liquidated in a group at a price which is less than the individual coins would bring, if sold one at a time. In these cases, exceptional investment values can be obtained. This is another case in which it is very favorable to have a continuing relationship with a professional numismatist, since these groups of coins are most often brought to a professional for liquidation. Having the relationship already established makes it possible to become part of this type of liquidation, to the benefit of all parties concerned.

Myth #8: It Was Once Legal To Produce Dollars outside The U.S. Mint.

This myth is part truth, part fiction. The actual case was that at one time in America's history it was legal to produce a dollar-*sized* coin. In other words, many of the expositions and special medals struck in the 18th and 19th Centuries were the size (diameter and thickness) of a U.S. silver dollar. However, technology made it impractical to allow this practice to continue.

As early as 1904, the advent of coin-operated vending machines made the use of medallions *exactly* the size of silver dollars impractical since they could be used as "slugs." The round Louisiana Purchase Exposition coin of admission had to be replaced with an octagonal coin due to its similarity to a silver dollar. "Slug" laws have been a concern to producers of special medallions ever since, which is one reason that few of these are the exact same size as silver dollars today, though many were before 1900.

Theory #8: There Are Silver Dollars Which Can Be Counterfeited.

This is an area of concern, particularly for the new investor in silver dollars, but very little of this problem actually arises in the coin industry in relation to the number of coins bought and sold. A few coins, as noted in Chapter 6, have been abused in this way in the past. However, if a professional numismatists is used as a consultant and guide by the investor, this problem *should never occur*. The key to successful silver dollar investing, in all ways, is a competent advisor who knows silver dollars thoroughly and can protect the investor from this type of problem.

Myth #9: The More Expensive The Better (In Terms Of Investment Potential).

All the reader has to do to see that this myth is untrue is review Chapter 6, with its many examples of lower priced coins which have been rated as better investments (in terms of potential return) than more expensive coins.

This is true for a wide variety of reasons, but in essence it all comes back to grading and pricing; each coin is individually graded and priced based on its own characteristics, its relation to original Mint State, the current demand and availability of the coins, etc. As a result, a $150 silver dollar in many cases is a better investment than a $10,000 silver dollar, simply because smaller increases in value will provide a higher relative return on the original purchase price.

Theory # 9: Cleaning Coins Will Improve Their Value.

This chapter began with a myth that "shinier is better," and will end with this discussion of cleaning coins.

For decades most people have been unsatisfied with the original mint state condition of coins, resulting in a nearly uncontrollable desire to clean them and "make them prettier." This is a grave mistake in many cases, particularly when someone who is not an expert attempts to clean an expensive coin.

While I am not saying that it is *always* a bad idea to clean a coin, I am saying that it is *usually* not a good idea. In a majority of cases, the desire to clean a coin is based on the incorrect assumption that it will somehow improve its value; usually the opposite occurs.

Coins have been cleaned in a variety of ways in the past: use of an abrasive; application of polish; buffing on a cloth wheel; using a household product that "restores gold, silver or copper to its original condition"; acid or corrosive bathing which causes obvious etching on the surfaces of the coin; submerging the coins in mercury which temporarily results in a high gloss, but later becomes a very dull finish, etc., etc., etc.

All of these methods result in damage to the coin; and the inevitable result of damaging a coin is a reduction in its value. In extreme cases, the coin's value is so badly harmed that it reverts to its near intrinsic value only. To a novice the coin may look temporarily improved, but to a professional numismatist, it is a disaster, that is *not* desirable.

A comparison that helps coin investors resist the temptation to "improve a coin's looks," is with a famous painting. Obviously, if you owned a famous painting, you would not consider using chemicals to "improve" it. The same is true of a rare piece of crystal. No one who owned a famous piece of lead crystal would consider washing it in an automatic dishwasher. If you owned a very rare bottle of wine, you wouldn't consider storing it out in the sunlight.

The same is true for coins. By exercising a reasonable amount of *common sense,* your coin investment can be preserved and enhanced.

In terms of maintenance, most coins are stored in plastic holders today. This is usually all of the maintenance required for silver dollars. The only other consideration is to store your coins in as dry an environment as possible; moisture can lead to corrosion, just as it does on sterling silver table settings.

If you store your coins in a personal depository or safe, it is possible to buy products that will maintain the interior environment at a very dry level. In other cases, the depository itself has a controlled temperature and humidity.

If a coin should begin to "tone" after you purchase it, "leave it be." There is nothing wrong with originally-toned coins. As discussed in the chapter on Grading (4), toning may actually add to the value of coins for some investors; and at the very least, it causes no change in value whatsoever. The only variety of toning which is negative to the value of the coin is a tone that is added *artificially*.

Again, the most important thing to remember about cleaning coins is that it is at best unnecessary, and at worst, extremely harmful to the value of the coin. It is common in the coin industry to consider coins that have been artificially cleaned or toned with extreme suspicion: most often it is taken as an effort to hide some defect or alteration in the coin, and the value of the coin is therefore greatly reduced.

ABSORPTION POINT GRAPH

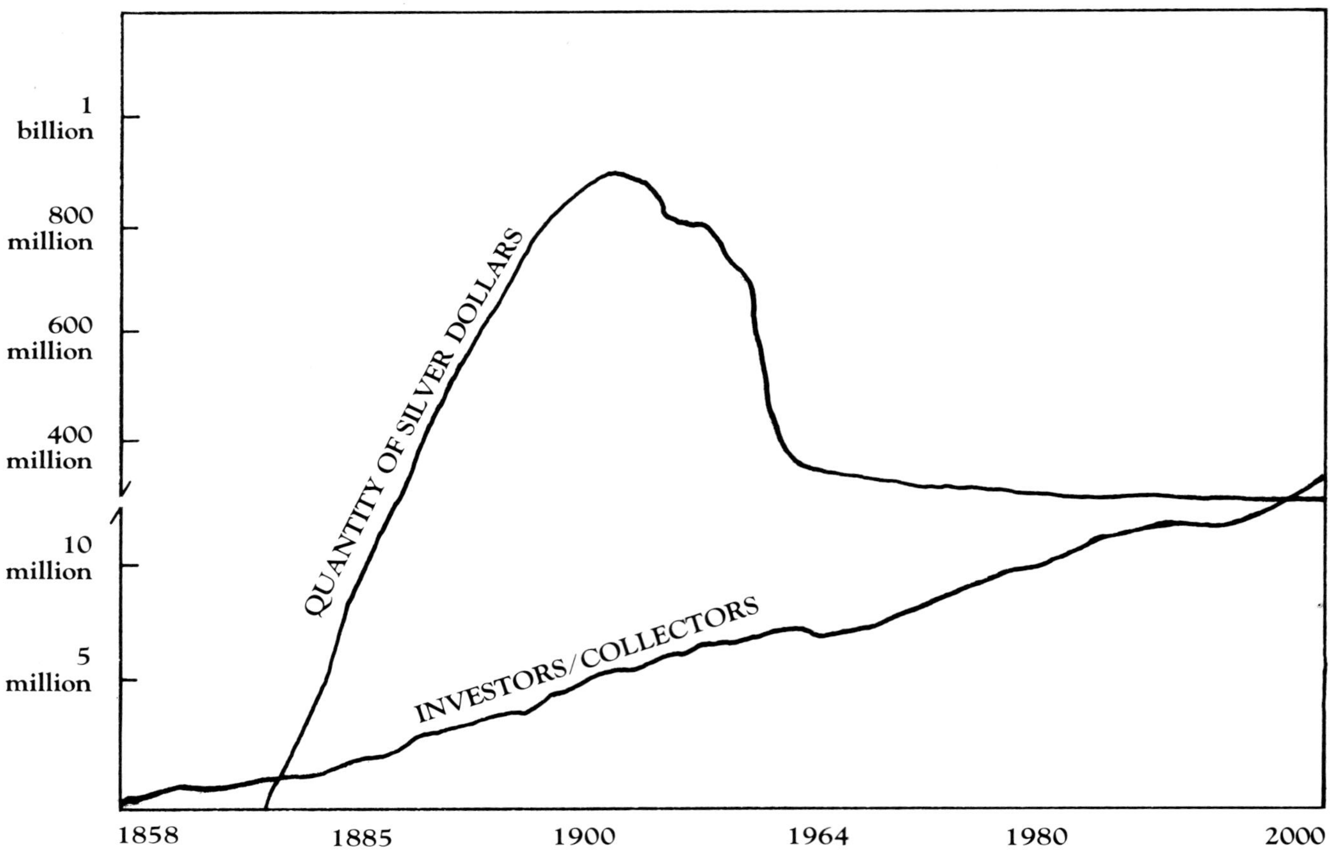

This chart demonstrates the number of silver dollars produced, minus the quantity melted, compared to the number of collectors and investors in silver dollars.

9

A GUIDE TO PROFESSIONAL NUMISMATICS

Introduction:

While the reader may have, by now, the impression that this author considers himself the only true professional in the field of numismatic investments, this is not the case at all.

Like all other professionals in a given industry, I continue to learn new lessons each day regarding the intricate details of my field; at nearly every auction and convention there are previously unknown coins, and new people in our industry who provide one more piece of information that helps make the entire picture of numismatics just a little clearer.

Realistically there are other professional numismatists in this country who subscribe to the principles outlined in the previous chapters, or who have the experience and capabilities to provide accurate information and consultations to investors.

There is a choice of hundreds of coin dealers available for the new investor, and quite a few offer the experience and ability I would recommend to readers. The list below is composed entirely of individuals and firms which I consider fine examples of professional numismatists. These are people and companies that I have dealt with myself, and I know from my own personal experience over nearly two decades in this industry that these individuals are truthful in their dealings; they are accurate in their grading and pricing, and they stand behind the products they sell with their own personal guarantees of authenticity and accuracy.

This is not to say that we agree at all times, and on all topics. However our basic principles are the same. Categorically, these individuals make a concerted, professional effort to provide the highest level of service possible for their clients.

These individuals share a number of basic characteristics which are considered crucial in determining the professionalism of a numismatist. These characteristics include many years of extensive experience in terms of buying and selling coins; access to state-of-the-art technology to provide them with the time required to remain up-to-the-minute on trends in our industry; attendance at most major shows and auctions each year; and, finally, these individuals invest in gem-quality silver dollars themselves.

This last point is extremely important when considering how to select a numismatic advisor, whether you are just beginning to invest in silver dollars, or you have years of experience. While many of these professional numismatists also buy and sell other numismatic items, all have extensive personal experience in silver dollar investments. In addition, all agree in principle with the basic recommendations for silver dollar investments outlined in the previous chapters.

While their lifestyles vary as much as their geographic locations, all are affluent people who have experience in handling very large transactions. They will also take time to introduce a new investor to the basic considerations of rare silver dollar investments. These are full service numismatists who can handle other needs for their clients in addition to silver dollar consultations and investments.

Finally, these professional numismatists are leaders in the numismatic industry; they are actively involved in setting the "style" of the industry, as well as proposing and executing advancements in our industry which are required to meet the changing nature of the numismatic marketplace. They are active in major associations and organizations within the numismatic field which guide the growth and development of this century-old profession.

In selecting one of these professional numismatists, two additional considerations are important: geography and personality. Obviously, it is not practical for any numismatist to handle the needs of all of the investors nationwide and around the world. While I do advise clients who are scattered geographically all around the globe, some investors prefer their numismatic advisor to be from more or less the same geographic area, simply for convenience, if for no other considerations. As a result, the list that follows represents as broad a geographic spread of the United States as possible within the professional guidelines listed previously.

Second, as stated above, there is a wide variety of lifestyles and personalities represented in the list of people that are recommended as professional numismatists. If it is feasible, new investors should meet and interview the professional numismatist they are considering as their own personal advisor. This will tell the client a great deal about that firm's operations and "style." In addition, it will provide an experience with the numismatist upon which to determine the client's desire and ability to deal with that individual or firm on a continuing basis. I believe that numismatic investing should be a very pleasant, very enjoyable experience, as well as a very rewarding one.

PROMINENT NUMISMATISTS WITH EXTENSIVE EXPERIENCE IN SILVER DOLLAR INVESTMENTS

Dick A. Reed
Metro Coin, Ltd.
4455 E. Camelback Rd.,
Suite A 115
Phoenix, Arizona 85018

Harlan White
Old Coin Shop
2425 El Cajon Blvd.
San Diego, California 92104

James U. Blanchard
James U. Blanchard & Co., Inc.
Security Center, Fourth Floor
147 Carondelet Street
New Orleans, Louisiana 70130

Dean Tavenner
Dean Tavenner Rare Coins
427 Main Street
P.O. Box 231
Deer Lodge, Montana 59722

Dennis Steinmetz
Steinmetz Coins & Currency
843 Park City Center
Lancaster, Pennsylvania 17601

John Highfill
Oklahoma Federated Gold & Numismatics, Inc.
P.O. Box 45849
Tulsa, Oklahoma 74145

Daryl Mercer
Tebo Coin Company
2863 28th Street
P.O. Box 4900
Boulder, Colorado 80306

Nick Buzolich
Quality Coin Exchange, Inc.
19225 Ventura Blvd.
P.O. Box 392
Tarzana, California 91356

Hannes Tulving
Hannes Tulving Rare Coin Investments
4400 MacArthur Blvd.
Suite 320
Newport Beach, California 92660

Mike DeFalco
Mike DeFalco Rare Coins
554 E. Foothill Blvd.
Suite 107
San Dimas, California 91773

Dennis Baker
The Coin Show
1021 N. Sepulveda Blvd., No. F-6
Manhattan Beach, California 90266

Thomas Tkacz
GlenRock Coin Shop
206½ Rock Road
Glen Rock, New Jersey 07452

APPENDIX A

QUANTITY MINTED IN DATE AND MINT ORDER

Date	Quantity
1878, 8 tail feathers	750,000
1878, 7 tail feathers	9,759,550
1878, 7 over 8 feathers	N/A
1878S	9,774,000
1878CC	2,212,000
1879	14,807,100
1879O	2,887,000
1879S	9,110,000
1879CC	756,000
1880	12,601,355
1880O	5,305,000
1880S	8,900,000
1880CC	591,000
1881	9,163,975
1881O	5,708,000
1881S	12,760,000
1881CC	296,000
1882	11,101,100
1882O	6,090,000
1882S	9,250,000
1882CC	1,133,000
1883	12,291,039
1883O	8,725,000
1883S	6,250,000
1883CC	1,204,000
1884	14,070,875
1884O	9,730,000
1884S	3,200,000
1884CC	1,136,000
1885	17,787,767
1885O	9,185,000
1885S	1,497,000
1885CC	228,000
1886	19,963,886
1886O	10,710,000
1886S	750,000
1887	20,290,710
1887O	11,550,000
1887S	1,771,000
1888	19,183,333
1888O	12,150,000
1888S	657,000
1889	21,726,811
1889O	11,875,000
1889S	700,000
1889CC	350,000
1890	16,802,590
1890O	10,701,000
1890S	8,230,373
1890CC	2,309,041
1891	8,694,206
1891O	7,954,529

Date	Quantity
1891S	5,296,000
1891CC	1,618,000
1892	1,037,245
1892O	2,744,000
1892S	1,200,000
1892CC	1,352,000
1893	389,792
1893O	300,000
1893S	100,000
1893CC	677,000
1894	110,972
1894O	1,723,000
1894S	1,260,000
1895	12,880
1895O	450,000
1895S	400,000
1896	9,976,762
1896O	4,900,000
1896S	5,000,000
1897	2,822,731
1897O	4,004,000
1897S	5,825,000
1898	5,884,735
1898O	4,440,000
1898S	4,102,000
1899	330,846
1899O	12,290,000
1899S	2,562,000
1900	8,830,912
1900O	12,590,000
1900S	3,540,000
1901	6,962,813
1901O	13,320,000
1901S	2,284,000
1902	7,994,777
1902O	8,636,000
1902S	1,530,000
1903	4,652,755
1903O	4,450,000
1903S	1,241,000
1904	2,788,650
1904O	3,720,000
1904S	2,304,000
1921	44,690,000
1921D	20,345,000
1921S	21,695,000

PEACE DOLLARS

Date	Quantity
1921	1,006,473
1922	51,737,000
1922D	15,063,000
1922S	17,475,000
1923	30,800,000
1923D	6,811,000
1923S	19,020,000
1924	11,811,000
1924S	1,728,000
1925	10,198,000
1925S	1,610,000
1926	1,939,000

1926D	2,348,700
1926S	6,980,000
1927	848,000
1927D	1,268,900
1927S	866,000
1928	360,649
1928S	1,632,000
1934	954,057
1934D	1,569,500
1934S	1,011,000
1935	1,576,000
1935S	1,964,000

APPENDIX B

QUANTITY OF DOLLARS MINTED BY YEAR

Year	Quantity
1878	22,495,550
1879	27,560,100
1880	27,397,355
1881	27,927,975
1882	27,574,100
1883	28,470,039
1884	28,136,875
1885	28,697,766
1886	31,423,886
1887	33,611,710
1888	31,990,833
1889	34,651,811
1890	38,043,004
1891	23,562,735
1892	6,333,245
1893	1,455,792
1894	3,093,972
1895	862,880
1896	19,876,762
1897	12,651,731
1898	14,426,735
1899	15,182,846
1900	24,960,912
1901	22,566,813
1902	18,160,777
1903	10,343,755
1904	8,812,650
1921	86,730,000

PEACE DOLLARS

Year	Quantity
1921	1,006,473
1922	84,275,000
1923	56,631,000
1924	13,539,000
1925	11,808,000
1926	11,267,700
1927	2,982,900
1928	1,992,649
1934	3,534,557
1935	3,540,000

APPENDIX C

QUANTITY PRODUCED BY MINT

Philadelphia

Year	Quantity
1895	12,880
1894	110,972
1899	330,846
1893	378,792
1892	1,037,245
1904	2,788,650
1897	2,822,731
1903	4,652,755
1898	5,884,735
1901	6,962,813
1902	7,994,777
1891	8,694,206
1900	8,830,912
1881	9,163,975
1896	9,976,762
1878 (All Types)	10,509,550
1882	11,101,100
1883	12,291,039
1880	12,601,355
1884	14,070,875
1879	14,807,100
1890	16,802,590
1885	17,787,767
1888	19,183,833
1886	19,963,886
1887	20,290,710
1889	21,726,811
1921	44,690,000

New Orleans

Year	Quantity
1893O	300,000
1895O	450,000
1894O	1,723,000
1892O	2,744,000
1879O	2,887,000
1904O	3,720,000
1897O	4,004,000
1898O	4,440,000
1903O	4,450,000
1896O	4,900,000
1880O	5,305,000
1881O	5,708,000
1882O	6,090,000
1891O	7,954,529
1902O	8,636,000
1883O	8,725,000
1885O	9,185,000
1884O	9,730,000
1890O	10,701,000
1886O	10,710,000

1887O	11,550,000
1889O	11,875,000
1888O	12,150,000
1899O	12,290,000
1900O	12,590,000
1901O	13,320,000
San Francisco	
1893S	100,000
1895S	400,000
1888S	657,000
1889S	700,000
1886S	750,000
1892S	1,200,000
1903S	1,241,000
1894S	1,260,000
1885S	1,497,000
1902S	1,530,000
1887S	1,771,000
1901S	2,284,000
1904S	2,304,000
1899S	2,562,000
1884S	3,200,000
1900S	3,540,000
1898S	4,102,000
1896S	5,000,000
1891S	5,296,000
1897S	5,825,000
1883S	6,250,000
1890S	8,230,373
1880S	8,900,000
1879S	9,110,000
1882S	9,250,000
1878S	9,774,000
1881S	12,760,000
1921S	21,695,000
Carson City	
1885CC	228,000
1881CC	296,000
1899CC	350,000
1880CC	591,000
1893CC	677,000
1879CC	756,000
1882CC	1,133,000
1884CC	1,136,000
1883CC	1,204,000
1892CC	1,352,000
1891CC	1,618,000
1878CC	2,212,000
1890CC	2,309,041
Denver	
1921D	20,345,000

PEACE DOLLARS

Philadelphia	
1928	360,649
1927	848,000
1934	954,057
1921	1,006,473
1935	1,576,000
1926	1,939,000
1925	10,198,000
1924	11,811,000
1923	30,800,000

1922 51,737,000

Denver

1927D 1,268,900

1934D 1,569,500

1926D 2,348,700

1923D 6,811,000

1922D 15,063,000

San Francisco

1927S 866,000

1934S 1,011,000

1925S 1,610,000

1928S 1,632,000

1924S 1,728,000

1935S 1,964,000

1926S 6,980,000

1922S 17,475,000

1923S 19,020,000

APPENDIX D

QUANTITY MINTED IN INCREASING ORDER

Date	Quantity
1895	12,880
1893S	100,000
1894	110,972
1885CC	228,000
1881CC	296,000
1893O	300,000
1899	330,846
1889CC	350,000
1893	378,792
1895S	400,000
1895O	450,000
1880CC	591,000
1888S	657,000
1893CC	677,000
1889S	700,000
1886S	750,000
1879CC	756,000
1892	1,037,245
1882CC	1,133,000
1884CC	1,136,000
1892S	1,200,000
1883CC	1,204,000
1903S	1,241,000
1894S	1,260,000
1892CC	1,352,000
1885S	1,497,000
1902S	1,530,000
1891CC	1,618,000
1894O	1,723,000
1887S	1,771,000
1878CC	2,212,000
1901S	2,284,000
1904S	2,304,000
1890CC	2,309,041
1899S	2,562,000
1892O	2,744,000
1904	2,788,650
1897	2,822,731
1879O	2,887,000
1884S	3,200,000
1900S	3,540,000
1904O	3,720,000
1897O	4,004,000
1898S	4,102,000
1898O	4,440,000
1903O	4,450,000
1903	4,652,755
1896O	4,900,000
1896S	5,000,000
1891S	5,296,000

1880O	5,305,000	1890O	10,701,000
1881O	5,708,000	1886O	10,710,000
1897S	5,825,000	1882	11,101,100
1898	5,884,735	1887O	11,550,000
1882O	6,090,000	1889O	11,875,000
1883S	6,250,000	1888O	12,150,000
1901	6,962,813	1899O	12,290,000
1891O	7,954,529	1883	12,291,039
1902	7,994,777	1900O	12,590,000
1890S	8,230,373	1880	12,601,355
1902O	8,636,000	1881S	12,760,000
1891	8,694,206	1901O	13,320,000
1883O	8,725,000	1884	14,070,875
1900	8,830,912	1879	14,807,100
1880S	8,900,000	1890	16,802,590
1879S	9,110,000	1885	17,787,767
1881	9,163,975	1888	19,183,833
1885O	9,185,000	1886	19,963,886
1882S	9,250,000	1887	20,290,710
1884O	9,730,000	1921D	20,345,000
1878S	9,774,000	1921S	21,695,000
1896	9,976,762	1889	21,726,811
1878 (All Types)	10,509,550	1921	44,690,000

PEACE DOLLARS

1928	360,649	1934D	1,569,500
1927	848,000	1935	1,576,000
1927S	866,000	1925S	1,610,000
1934	954,057	1928S	1,632,000
1921	1,006,473	1924S	1,728,000
1934S	1,011,000	1926	1,939,000
1927D	1,268,900	1935S	1,964,000

1926D	2,348,700
1923D	6,811,000
1926S	6,980,000
1925	10,198,000
1924	11,811,000
1922D	15,063,000
1922S	17,475,000
1923S	19,020,000
1923	30,800,000
1922	51,737,000

APPENDIX E

REVERSE ORDER OF QUANTITY MINTED

Date	Quantity
1921	44,690,000
1889	21,726,811
1921S	21,695,000
1921D	20,345,000
1887	20,290,710
1886	19,963,886
1888	19,183,833
1885	17,787,767
1890	16,802,590
1879	14,807,100
1884	14,070,875
1901O	13,320,000
1881S	12,760,000
1880	12,601,355
1900O	12,590,000
1883	12,291,039
1899O	12,290,000
1888O	12,150,000
1889O	11,875,000
1887O	11,550,000
1882	11,101,100
1886O	10,710,000
1890O	10,701,000
1878 (All Types)	10,509,550
1896	9,976,762
1878S	9,774,000
1884O	9,730,000
1882S	9,250,000
1885O	9,185,000
1881	9,163,975
1879S	9,110,000
1880S	8,900,000
1900	8,830,912
1883O	8,725,000
1891	8,694,206
1902O	8,636,000
1890S	8,230,373
1902	7,994,777
1891O	7,954,529
1901	6,962,813
1883S	6,250,000
1882O	6,090,000
1898	5,884,735
1897S	5,825,000
1881O	5,708,000
1880O	5,305,000
1891S	5,296,000
1896S	5,000,000
1896O	4,900,000
1903	4,652,755

Date	Quantity
1903O	4,450,000
1898O	4,440,000
1898S	4,102,000
1897O	4,004,000
1904O	3,720,000
1900S	3,540,000
1884S	3,200,000
1879O	2,887,000
1897	2,822,731
1904	2,788,650
1892O	2,744,000
1899S	2,562,000
1890CC	2,309,041
1904S	2,304,000
1901S	2,284,000
1878CC	2,212,000
1887S	1,771,000
1894O	1,723,000
1891CC	1,618,000
1902S	1,530,000
1885S	1,497,000
1892CC	1,352,000
1894S	1,260,000
1903S	1,241,000
1883CC	1,204,000
1892S	1,200,000
1884CC	1,136,000
1882CC	1,133,000
1892	1,037,245
1879CC	756,000
1886S	750,000
1889S	700,000
1893CC	677,000
1888S	657,000
1880CC	591,000
1895O	450,000
1895S	400,000
1893	378,792
1889CC	350,000
1899	330,846
1893O	300,000
1881CC	296,000
1885CC	228,000
1894	110,972
1893S	100,000
1895	12,880

PEACE DOLLARS

Date	Quantity
1922	51,737,000
1923	30,800,000
1923S	19,020,000
1922S	17,475,000
1922D	15,063,000
1924	11,811,000
1925	10,198,000
1926S	6,980,000
1923D	6,811,000
1926D	2,348,700
1935S	1,964,000
1926	1,939,000

1924S	1,728,000
1928S	1,632,000
1925S	1,610,000
1935	1,576,000
1934D	1,569,500
1927D	1,268,900
1934S	1,011,000
1921	1,006,473
1934	954,057
1927S	866,000
1927	848,000
1928	360,649

APPENDIX F

MORGAN SILVER DOLLAR DIES PRODUCED

*Fiscal Year**	Philadelphia	New Orleans	San Francisco	Carson City
1903	142	180	20	†
1902	136	300	40	†
1901	114	210	80	†
1900	45	230	40	†
1899	37	140	40	†
1898	40	34	58	†
1897	70	50	98	†
1896	40	40	40	†
1895	4	10	38	†
1894	††	20	20	†
1893	16	20	30	20
1892	15	30	33	30
1891	81	100	73	40
1890	95	60	80	50
1889	104	150	20	10
1888	116	136	80	†
1887	107	108	8	†
1886	161	80	††	†
1885	131	124	40	20
1884	128	60	80	20
1883	127	92	105	20
1882	92	50	80	30
1881	148	119	200	50
1880	199	80	110	25
1879	157	40	192	30
1878	92	†	192	100
TOTAL	2,397	2,463	1,797	445

*These statistics were taken from statistics of the director of the Bureau of the U.S. Mint and are based on the fiscal year beginning July 1 and ending June 30. As a result, these figures do not represent the number of die varieties to produce coins by calendar year.

† None minted
†† Not available

APPENDIX G

AVAILABILITY OF MS-60 AND ABOVE COINS BY DATE

Date	Number
1878-8TF	23,800
1878-7TF	28,150
1878-7/8TF	22,825
1878S	587,000
1878CC	102,250
1879	72,900
1879O	34,550
1879S	587,000
1879CC	12,405
1880	119,075
1880O	18,250
1880S	1,064,500
1880CC	172,250
1881	91,000
1881O	75,750
1881S	1,183,500
1881CC	210,500
1882	80,655
1882O	115,150
1882S	889,500
1882CC	717,500
1883	110,900
1883O	692,200
1883S	8,745
1883CC	824,800
1884	56,950
1884O	668,900
1884S	714
1884CC	1,117,000
1885	850,400
1885O	682,900
1885S	31,360
1885CC	207,250
1886	698,220
1886O	11,560
1886S	21,275
1887	725,200
1887O	65,535
1887S	38,200
1888	178,250
1888O	121,120
1888S	22,245
1889	207,925
1889O	69,050
1889S	21,485
1889CC	2,845
1890	115,225
1890O	43,750
1890S	107,550
1890CC	42,650

Date	Mintage	Date	Mintage
1891	25,375	1898	233,600
1891O	10,490	1898O	545,590
1891S	114,425	1898S	20,925
1891CC	20,730	1899	39,305
1892	9,585	1899O	347,250
1892O	2,596	1899S	16,295
1892S	789	1900	157,865
1892CC	13,401	1900O	327,025
1893	5,692	1900S	26,750
1893O	2,007	1901	1,834
1893S	203	1901O	366,300
1893CC	8,970	1901S	11,255
1894	3,644	1902	21,465
1894O	4,378	1902O	348,620
1894S	11,463	1902S	10,040
1895	747	1903	68,500
1895O	1,901	1903O	67,750
1895S	6,540	1903S	5,915
1896	146,800	1904	33,210
1896O	5,876	1904O	852,000
1896S	9,863	1904S	12,250
1897	78,410	1921	5,062,500
1897O	10,800	1921D	76,100
1897S	68,505	1921S	68,835

PEACE DOLLARS

Date	Mintage	Date	Mintage
1921	32,115	1923D	86,300
1922	6,487,850	1923S	60,563
1922D	39,845	1924	503,675
1922S	58,572	1924S	24,265
1923	4,216,000	1925	408,000

Date	Number	Date	Number
1925S	43,508	1928	16,850
1926	75,500	1928S	12,222
1926D	176,050	1934	27,380
1926S	48,675	1934D	20,250
1927	16,768	1934S	5,709
1927D	30,960	1935	55,240
1927S	8,635	1935S	29,115

APPENDIX H

AVAILABILITY OF MS-60 AND ABOVE COINS IN QUANTITY ORDER

Date	Quantity
1893S	203
1884S	714
1895	747
1892S	789
1901	1,834
1895O	1,901
1893O	2,007
1892O	2,596
1889CC	2,845
1894	3,644
1894O	4,378
1893	5,692
1896O	5,876
1903S	5,915
1895S	6,540
1883S	8,745
1893CC	8,970
1892	9,585
1896S	9,863
1902S	10,040
1891O	10,490
1897O	10,800
1901S	11,255
1894S	11,463
1886O	11,560
1904S	12,250
1879CC	12,405
1892CC	13,401
1899S	16,295
1880O	18,250
1891CC	20,730
1898S	20,925
1886S	21,275
1902	21,465
1889S	21,485
1888S	22,245
1878-7/8TF	22,825
1878-8TF	23,800
1891	25,375
1900S	26,750
1878-7TF	28,150
1885S	31,360
1904	33,210
1879O	34,550
1887S	38,200
1899	39,305
1890CC	42,650
1890O	43,750
1884	56,950

1887O	65,535
1903O	67,750
1903	68,500
1897S	68,505
1921S	68,835
1889O	69,050
1879	72,900
1881O	75,750
1921D	76,100
1897	78,410
1882	80,655
1881	91,000
1878CC	102,250
1890S	107,550
1883	110,900
1891S	114,425
1882O	115,150
1890	115,225
1880	119,075
1888O	121,120
1896	146,800
1900	157,865
1880CC	172,250
1888	178,250
1885CC	207,250
1889	207,925
1881CC	210,500
1898	233,600
1900O	327,025
1899O	347,250
1902O	348,620
1901O	366,300
1898O	545,590
1878S	587,000
1879S	587,000
1884O	668,900
1885O	682,900
1883O	692,200
1886	698,220
1882CC	717,500
1887	725,200
1883CC	824,800
1885	850,400
1904O	852,000
1882S	889,500
1880S	1,064,500
1884CC	1,117,000
1881S	1,183,500
1921	5,062,500

PEACE DOLLARS

1934S	5,709
1927S	8,635
1928S	12,222
1927	16,768
1928	16,850
1934D	20,250
1924S	24,265
1934	27,380

1935S	29,115
1927D	30,960
1921	32,115
1922D	39,845
1925S	43,508
1926S	48,675
1935	55,240
1922S	58,572
1923S	60,563
1926	75,500
1923D	86,300
1926D	176,050
1925	408,000
1924	503,675
1923	4,216,000
1922	6,487,850

APPENDIX I

Coins Actively Traded in Rolls (MS-63 or higher grades)

Morgan	1882-S	1886-P	1897-P	1900-O	**Peace**
1878-S	1883-O	1887-P	1898-P	1901-O	1922-P
1879-S	1884-O	1888-P	1898-O	1902-O	1923-P
1880-S	1885-P	1889-P	1899-O	1904-O	1924-P
1881-S	1885-O	1896-P	1900-P	1921-P	1925-P

Coins Actively Traded as Single Coins*

Morgan	1881-O	1886-S**	1891-P	1902-P**	1925-S
1878-7	1881-CC	1887-O	1891-O**	1903-P	1926-P
1878-8	1882-P	1887-S	1891-S	1903-O	1926-D
1878-7/8	1882-O	1888-O	1891-CC	1921-D	1926-S
1878-CC	1882-CC	1888-S**	1892-P**	1921-S	1928-P
1879-P	1883-P	1889-O**	1892-CC**	**Peace**	1934-P
1879-O	1883-CC	1889-S	1897-S	1922-D**	1934-D**
1880-P	1884-P	1890-P	1898-S**	1922-S**	1934-S
1880-O	1884-CC	1890-O**	1899-P	1923-D	1935-P**
1880-CC	1885-S**	1890-S	1899-S**	1923-S**	1935-S**
1881-P	1885-CC	1890-CC	1900-S**		

Coins Seldom Offered in Quantities of Two or More

Morgans	1892-O	1894-P	1896-O	1903-S	1924-S
1879-CC	1892-S	1894-O	1896-S	1904-P	1927-P
1883-S	1893-P	1894-S	1897-O	1904-S	1927-D
1884-S	1893-O	1895-P	1901-P	**Peace**	1927-S
1886-O	1893-S	1895-O	1901-S	1921-P	1928-S
1889-CC	1893-CC	1895-S	1902-S		

* Twenty years ago, *all* coins were offered in rolls with about eight exceptions that traded exclusively as singles.
** Border line availability in groups of single coins.

APPENDIX J

SILVER DOLLARS MELTED BY FISCAL YEAR

Year	Amount	Year	Amount	Year	Amount
1964	1,293,378	1936	638	1908	1,170
1963	1,080,724	1935	649	1907	1,548
1962	333,175	1934	504	1906	909
1961	196,520	1933	513	1905	2,298
1960	191,585	1932	442	1904	1,304
1959	332,669	1931	1,193	1903	1,777
1958	190,531	1930	1,329	1902	1,893
1957	216,481	1929	852	1901	1,786
1956	1,700,211	1928	1,394	1900	1,341
1955	669,317	1927	3,638	1899	1,734
1954	498,034	1926	2,594	1898	1,365
1953	378,993	1925	1,773	1897	1,898
1952	351,642	1924	1,918	1896	2,034
1951	334,439	1923	2,635	1895	18,580
1950	274,623	1922	2,447	1894	15,055
1949	242,666	1921	113,064	1893	10,500
1948	362,240	1920	10,001,164	1892	42,881
1947	688,946	1919	191,370,031	1891	10,800
1946	97,072	1918	68,753,583	1890	11,977
1945	394,317	1917	961	1889	31,642
1944	44,658,876	1916	1,092	1888	14,055
1943	8,080,983	1915	823	1887	8,292
1942	562	1914	785	1886	0
1941	407	1913	4,757	1885	1,850
1940	366	1912	1,024	1884	0
1939	629	1911	1,320	1883	621
1938	607	1910	961	TOTAL	333,022,048
1937	339	1909	1,293		

*These statistics were taken from the statistics of the Director of the Bureau of the U.S. Mint and are based on the fiscal year beginning July 1 and ending June 30.

APPENDIX K

Update Subscriptions

Update is published monthly by Metro Coin, Ltd. of Phoenix, Arizona, U.S.A. and is available worldwide to investors in gem-quality coins and stamps at a subscription rate of $100 (U.S. or equivalent) per year.

Update offers the latest news in coin and stamp collecting, reviews of current market conditions, recommendations regarding undervalued coins and stamps, and the personal views and recommendations of Dick A. Reed, one of America's foremost experts on collecting and investing in gem-quality rare coins. To subscribe, send $100 in check or money order to:

Metro Coin, Ltd.
4455 East Camelback Road, Suite 115A
Phoenix, Arizona U.S.A. 85018

YES*, I want to subscribe to *Update*. Please send my issues to:

Name ______________________ Phone (   ) ______________________

Address ____

City ______________ State ______________ Zip __________

I have enclosed my ☐ check ☐ money order for $100.

Send to: Metro Coin, Ltd.
4455 East Camelback Road, Suite 115A
Phoenix, Arizona U.S.A. 85018

---

*Please photocopy this form and send with your check to subscribe.

APPENDIX L

American Numismatic Association
P.O. Box 2366
Colorado Springs, CO 80901

Application for Membership***

Check One: ☐ Regular ☐ Junior ☐ Associate ☐ Life ☐ Club

Present or former no., if any ______________

☐ Mr. ☐ Mrs. ☐ Miss ☐ Club

Name ______________
(Please Print and Use First Name)

Street ______________

City ______________ State ______________ Zip ______________

Birthdate ______________ Occupation ______________

ANA Bylaws require the publication of each application. If you DO NOT wish your STREET address published, please check this box ☐

I herewith make application for membership in the American Numismatic Association, subject to the Bylaws of said Association. I also agree to abide by the Code of Ethics adopted by the Association.

Signature of Applicant ______________ Date ______________

Signature of Proposer ______________ ANA No. LM 1490

Signature of Proposer ______________
(Parent or Guardian must sign for Junior applicants)

☐ Master Charge ☐ Visa Account No. ______________ Expiration Date ______________

DUES

Regular (U.S. only)

☐ 1 Year - $15* ☐ 3 Years - $40* ☐ 5 Years - $60*

Regular (all other countries) 18*
Club (wherever located) 15*
Junior (11-17 years old) 9
Associate (child or spouse of R or LM) 2

Life (adult individual) 350
(Installment, $60 with application**, plus $25 per month for 12 months)
Life (club) 1000

* Add $5 application fee, first year only
** Includes $10 bookkeeping fee, deducted from final payment if made within 90 days of application. Life Membership is not effective until full $350 fee is paid.

***Please photocopy this form and send to ANA.

Note: To be used as a continuing record of silver dollar investments.

	MS-60	MS-63	MS-64	MS-65	MS-67	MS-69	PL-63	PL-65
Morgan								
1878								
1878S								
1878CC								
1879								
1879O								
1879S								
1879CC								
1880								
1880O								
1880S								
1880CC								
1881								
1881O								
1881S								
1881CC								
1882								
1882O								
1882S								
1882CC								
1883								
1883O								
1883S								
1883CC								
1884								
1884O								
1884S								
1884CC								
1885								
1885O								

	MS-60	MS-63	MS-64	MS-65	MS-67	MS-69	PL-63	PL-65
1885S								
1885CC								
1886								
1886O								
1886S								
1887								
1887O								
1887S								
1888								
1888O								
1888S								
1889								
1889O								
1889S								
1889CC								
1890								
1890O								
1890S								
1890CC								
1891								
1891O								
1891S								
1891CC								
1892								
1892O								
1892S								
1892CC								
1893								
1893O								
1893S								
1893CC								
1894								
1894O								

	MS-60	MS-63	MS-64	MS-65	MS-67	MS-69	PL-63	PL-65
1894S								
1895								
1895O								
1895S								
1896								
1896O								
1896S								
1897								
1897O								
1897S								
1898								
1898O								
1898S								
1899								
1899O								
1899S								
1900								
1900O								
1900S								
1901								
1901O								
1901S								
1902								
1902O								
1902S								
1903								
1903O								
1903S								
1904								
1904O								

	MS-60	MS-63	MS-64	MS-65	MS-67	MS-69	PL-63	PL-65
1904S								
1921								
1921D								
1921S								
Peace								
1921								
1922								
1922D								
1922S								
1923								
1923D								
1923S								
1924								
1924S								
1925								
1925S								
1926								
1926D								
1926S								
1927								
1927D								
1927S								
1928								
1928S								
1934								
1934D								
1934S								
1935								
1935S								

METRO COIN, LTD.
Wholesale Price Guide

YEAR	GRADE 60	63	64	65	67**	69**	PL 63	PL 65
1878-8	$50.00	$75.00	$150.00	$350.00	$700.00	$1,100.00	$125.00	$700.00
1878-7	35.00	60.00	200.00	450.00	675.00	800.00	100.00	550.00
1878⅞	50.00	100.00	375.00	700.00	1,100.00	1,800.00	100.00	950.00
1878-S	35.00	60.00	90.00	160.00	275.00	500.00	90.00	325.00
1878-CC	100.00	130.00	175.00	250.00	450.00	700.00	150.00	450.00
1879	30.00	60.00	200.00	500.00	850.00	1,300.00	100.00	750.00
1879-O	45.00	125.00	475.00	900.00	2,000.00	4,000.00	200.00	1,750.00
1879-S	35.00	60.00	90.00	145.00	250.00	450.00	85.00	310.00
1879-CC*	600.00	1,250.00	2,000.00	3,500.00	6,500.00	10,000.00	1,500.00	7,500.00
1880	30.00	60.00	170.00	400.00	775.00	1,100.00	100.00	700.00
1880-O	50.00	150.00	450.00	1,000.00	2,200.00	4,000.00	200.00	1,800.00
1880-S	35.00	60.00	90.00	145.00	250.00	475.00	75.00	340.00
1880-CC	140.00	200.00	265.00	350.00	625.00	950.00	250.00	600.00
1881	30.00	60.00	120.00	400.00	650.00	900.00	100.00	700.00
1881-O	30.00	60.00	175.00	425.00	725.00	1,100.00	90.00	700.00
1881-S	35.00	60.00	80.00	140.00	250.00	400.00	75.00	325.00
1881-CC	150.00	200.00	260.00	360.00	575.00	900.00	225.00	600.00
1882	30.00	60.00	125.00	375.00	600.00	900.00	100.00	700.00
1882-O	30.00	60.00	175.00	450.00	750.00	1,100.00	85.00	700.00
1882-S	35.00	60.00	80.00	180.00	275.00	475.00	90.00	400.00
1882-CC	65.00	80.00	120.00	175.00	275.00	675.00	100.00	450.00
1883	30.00	60.00	125.00	350.00	600.00	800.00	100.00	700.00
1883-O	30.00	45.00	85.00	185.00	250.00	500.00	85.00	350.00
1883-S	300.00	650.00	900.00	1,500.00	3,000.00	6,750.00	1,000.00	6,000.00
1883-CC	65.00	80.00	100.00	150.00	275.00	600.00	100.00	450.00
1884	30.00	70.00	175.00	425.00	600.00	1,000.00	150.00	800.00
1884-O	30.00	45.00	85.00	185.00	250.00	500.00	85.00	350.00
1884-S	650.00	2,500.00	4,500.00	9,000.00	15,000.00	40,000.00	4,000.00	13,000.00
1884-CC	65.00	80.00	100.00	150.00	275.00	600.00	100.00	450.00
1885	30.00	45.00	85.00	185.00	250.00	500.00	85.00	350.00
1885-O	30.00	45.00	85.00	185.00	250.00	500.00	85.00	350.00
1885-S	70.00	175.00	325.00	700.00	950.00	1,800.00	300.00	1,500.00
1885-CC	150.00	200.00	240.00	300.00	425.00	800.00	225.00	600.00
1886	30.00	45.00	85.00	150.00	250.00	500.00	80.00	350.00
1886-O	225.00	750.00	1,350.00	2,500.00	6,000.00	12,500.00	1,500.00	9,000.00
1886-S	80.00	200.00	350.00	550.00	900.00	1,500.00	220.00	1,000.00
1887	30.00	45.00	85.00	150.00	250.00	500.00	80.00	350.00
1887-O	35.00	100.00	250.00	650.00	1,000.00	2,000.00	150.00	1,400.00
1887-S	50.00	100.00	225.00	600.00	950.00	1,400.00	175.00	750.00
1888	30.00	50.00	150.00	350.00	600.00	875.00	100.00	600.00
1888-O	30.00	60.00	130.00	325.00	575.00	1,300.00	90.00	800.00
1888-S	100.00	200.00	325.00	500.00	950.00	1,400.00	225.00	1,000.00
1889	30.00	50.00	150.00	400.00	750.00	1,000.00	125.00	700.00
1889-O	50.00	250.00	575.00	1,500.00	4,000.00	6,500.00	350.00	3,500.00
1889-S	50.00	100.00	200.00	350.00	700.00	1,400.00	150.00	800.00
1889-CC	3,000.00	7,000.00	10,000.00	15,000.00	25,000.00	35,000.00	7,250.00	22,500.00
1890	30.00	70.00	175.00	500.00	900.00	1,400.00	175.00	850.00
1890-O	35.00	100.00	425.00	900.00	1,750.00	3,500.00	220.00	1,250.00
1890-S	35.00	75.00	120.00	225.00	475.00	750.00	100.00	450.00
1890-CC	175.00	275.00	400.00	600.00	950.00	1,350.00	300.00	850.00
1891	50.00	150.00	325.00	800.00	2,000.00	3,500.00	300.00	1,900.00
1891-O	60.00	175.00	625.00	1,700.00	4,250.00	9,000.00	1,000.00	7,000.00
1891-S	35.00	75.00	125.00	250.00	475.00	750.00	100.00	450.00
1891-CC	140.00	220.00	375.00	600.00	900.00	1,500.00	275.00	800.00
1892	100.00	300.00	625.00	1,200.00	2,100.00	3,500.00	450.00	3,000.00
1892-O	100.00	300.00	650.00	1,750.00	4,500.00	11,000.00	1,000.00	10,000.00
1892-S	3,000.00	6,500.00	9,500.00	15,000.00	23,000.00	37,500.00	8,000.00	25,000.00
1892-CC	250.00	400.00	525.00	750.00	1,400.00	2,200.00	475.00	1,500.00
1893	250.00	600.00	850.00	1,500.00	3,250.00	8,500.00	1,000.00	9,000.00
1893-O	750.00	2,000.00	4,500.00	9,000.00	17,500.00	30,000.00	7,000.00	25,000.00
1893-S	15,000.00	25,000.00	32,500.00	40,000.00	51,500.00	60,000.00	30,000.00	50,000.00

YEAR	GRADE 60	63	64	65	67**	69**	PL 63	PL 65
1893-CC	600.00	1,250.00	2,000.00	3,000.00	6,500.00	10,000.00	1,500.00	7,000.00
1894	650.00	1,400.00	2,200.00	3,500.00	6,000.00	11,000.00	5,500.00	10,000.00
1894-O	350.00	1,100.00	2,750.00	6,000.00	10,000.00	18,000.00	7,500.00	17,500.00
1894-S	250.00	700.00	1,100.00	1,500.00	3,250.00	6,000.00	800.00	4,000.00
1895 proof	10,000.00	13,000.00	15,500.00	20,000.00	25,000.00	30,000.00	—	—
1895-O	1,200.00	5,000.00	9,500.00	20,000.00	32,500.00	45,000.00	10,000.00	35,000.00
1895-S	650.00	1,400.00	2,100.00	3,000.00	4,250.00	8,000.00	1,600.00	7,000.00
1896	30.00	60.00	125.00	300.00	500.00	700.00	100.00	500.00
1896-O	600.00	1,500.00	4,000.00	8,000.00	17,500.00	30,000.00	6,500.00	20,000.00
1896-S	375.00	750.00	1,100.00	1,500.00	4,000.00	6,000.00	900.00	4,500.00
1897	30.00	75.00	175.00	400.00	675.00	900.00	125.00	600.00
1897-O	350.00	1,000.00	2,500.00	4,500.00	10,000.00	17,500.00	2,000.00	9,500.00
1897-S	40.00	100.00	165.00	275.00	525.00	750.00	100.00	550.00
1898	30.00	75.00	125.00	300.00	525.00	750.00	100.00	500.00
1898-O	30.00	65.00	125.00	285.00	500.00	700.00	90.00	400.00
1898-S	100.00	300.00	475.00	600.00	1,250.00	1,700.00	350.00	1,350.00
1899	60.00	175.00	300.00	500.00	875.00	1,300.00	200.00	975.00
1899-O	30.00	65.00	150.00	300.00	500.00	700.00	125.00	500.00
1899-S	125.00	300.00	450.00	600.00	1,000.00	1,600.00	350.00	1,400.00
1900	30.00	65.00	150.00	325.00	500.00	750.00	125.00	500.00
1900-O	30.00	65.00	150.00	300.00	500.00	750.00	120.00	500.00
1900-S	90.00	275.00	400.00	675.00	1,000.00	1,750.00	350.00	1,500.00
1901	600.00	2,000.00	4,500.00	10,000.00	16,000.00	23,000.00	6,500.00	20,000.00
1901-O	30.00	75.00	150.00	375.00	650.00	1,000.00	140.00	650.00
1901-S	175.00	400.00	875.00	1,750.00	3,000.00	5,000.00	700.00	4,000.00
1902	50.00	110.00	375.00	875.00	1,300.00	2,000.00	200.00	1,400.00
1902-O	30.00	60.00	175.00	325.00	550.00	800.00	135.00	500.00
1902-S	150.00	400.00	575.00	900.00	1,500.00	2,500.00	475.00	2,000.00
1903	40.00	100.00	200.00	375.00	700.00	1,000.00	175.00	750.00
1903-O	175.00	275.00	375.00	575.00	850.00	1,500.00	350.00	1,500.00
1903-S	1,000.00	2,300.00	4,000.00	6,000.00	9,500.00	15,000.00	3,000.00	12,500.00
1904	75.00	250.00	500.00	1,000.00	2,200.00	5,000.00	600.00	4,500.00
1904-O	30.00	60.00	160.00	275.00	400.00	650.00	100.00	400.00
1904-S	600.00	1,500.00	2,250.00	3,500.00	6,000.00	10,000.00	2,000.00	9,000.00
1921	25.00	35.00	65.00	165.00	275.00	400.00	100.00	350.00
1921-D	30.00	65.00	200.00	550.00	900.00	1,500.00	175.00	1,400.00
1921-S	30.00	80.00	300.00	800.00	1,500.00	4,000.00	300.00	4,000.00
1921	175.00	400.00	825.00	1,600.00	2,000.00	3,500.00		
1922	25.00	40.00	85.00	175.00	300.00	500.00		
1922-D	30.00	80.00	200.00	550.00	1,000.00	1,500.00		
1922-S	35.00	100.00	300.00	650.00	2,000.00	4,500.00		
1923	25.00	40.00	85.00	175.00	300.00	500.00		
1923-D	35.00	90.00	300.00	700.00	1,200.00	1,650.00		
1923-S	35.00	100.00	350.00	850.00	2,000.00	4,000.00		
1924	30.00	55.00	175.00	375.00	500.00	700.00		
1924-S	100.00	325.00	800.00	2,000.00	3,500.00	5,000.00		
1925	30.00	50.00	140.00	300.00	475.00	675.00		
1925-S	75.00	200.00	400.00	950.00	2,000.00	4,000.00		
1926	40.00	100.00	300.00	650.00	1,000.00	1,500.00		
1926-D	50.00	140.00	400.00	1,000.00	1,400.00	2,000.00		
1926-S	40.00	100.00	200.00	500.00	875.00	1,150.00		
1927	100.00	200.00	475.00	1,100.00	1,500.00	2,100.00		
1927-D	175.00	500.00	925.00	2,000.00	3,100.00	4,250.00		
1927-S	125.00	250.00	450.00	1,000.00	2,000.00	3,750.00		
1928	180.00	350.00	500.00	1,200.00	1,500.00	2,000.00		
1928-S	100.00	250.00	475.00	1,000.00	2,500.00	4,500.00		
1934	75.00	175.00	450.00	1,100.00	1,500.00	2,000.00		
1934-D	100.00	200.00	675.00	1,600.00	2,500.00	3,700.00		
1934-S	900.00	2,000.00	3,000.00	4,500.00	6,250.00	7,750.00		
1935	50.00	125.00	300.00	800.00	1,400.00	1,900.00		
1935-S	125.00	300.00	700.00	1,400.00	2,200.00	3,000.00		

* Price for regular 1879-CC, not "capped die" variety.

** Very seldom encounted.